Praise for
Rachel Wojo and *One More Step*

"In *One More Step,* Rachel Wojo gives p   world to grieve, ache, and experience sad   holding tight to their faith. It's refreshing to find a sister of the soul who doesn't offer platitudes but instead offers real life experience tangled in hope."

—SUZANNE ELLER, international speaker, blogger, and author
of numerous books including *The Mended Heart*

"We've all had situations in our lives where we just couldn't see how we'd make it through another day. With this book, you'll be encouraged and lifted up by Rachel, a friend who understands how to seek God's strength and healing in the midst of the pain!"

—LYSA TERKEURST, *New York Times* best-selling author and
president of Proverbs 31 Ministries

"This book is both personal and practical. Like our heavenly Father, Rachel is fluent in the language of pain. Anyone who has struggled or is struggling will find healing and hope on each page."

—JON WEECE, senior pastor and lead follower at Southland Christian
Church in Lexington, Kentucky, and author of *Jesus Prom*

"When you sit across from Rachel in real life and look in her eyes, you see a woman who wants nothing more than to please and know Jesus and give him away. Her passion for God is as contagious as it is sincere and no doubt built from much time in the trenches of suffering with him."

—JENNIE ALLEN, founder and CEO of IF:Gathering, and author
of *Restless* and *Anything*

"If your life circumstances have ever left you full of fear, dread, or worry, then this book is for you. Rachel is the friend who has been through life's cruel wringer and knows exactly how you feel. She gently shows you how to let God pull you out of the muck of life and point you back in the right—and righteous—direction. Encouraging and practical. This will be my new go-to book for hurting friends."

> —KAREN EHMAN, *New York Times* best-selling author and Proverbs 31 Ministries speaker

"Just when you think you can't go on, a friend who's been there offers you her hand. Rachel Wojo is a rare, beautiful writer who gets to the heart of the matter. In *One More Step,* Rachel writes honestly about pain but points to the beauty God wants to bring out of the broken places in our lives."

> —JOANNA WEAVER, author of *Having a Mary Heart in a Martha World*

"Rachel Wojo's personal journey, insights from her walk with Jesus, and hope-filled words make *One More Step* an encouraging guide for every heart when life's path gets rough."

> —HOLLEY GERTH, best-selling author of *You're Going to Be Okay* and *What Your Heart Needs for the Hard Days*

"Where do you turn when life simply feels too difficult to even keep going? Told with both wisdom and honesty, Rachel's story is equal parts heart-wrenching and encouraging. In the end, she offers a strong dose of hope for the hopeless and the strength to take just one more step."

> —RUTH SOUKUP, *New York Times* best-selling author of *Living Well, Spending Less*

"With down-to-earth honesty and soul-stirring inspiration, Rachel Wojo points our hearts toward lasting hope. She not only shares biblical truths we need to hear but shows us how to intentionally hold onto God's promises so we can walk confidently in his plans, no matter how hard life gets!"

> —RENEE SWOPE, best-selling author of *A Confident Heart* and radio co-host of Proverbs 31 Ministries' *Everyday Life with Lysa & Renee*

"Rachel combines powerful biblical truth with very real everyday life. If you're looking for help to simply take the next step, you will find it here."

> —SHEILA WALSH, author of *Five Minutes with Jesus*

one more step

RACHEL WOJO

one more step

Finding Strength
When You Feel Like Giving Up

WATERBROOK
PRESS

One More Step
Published by WaterBrook Press
12265 Oracle Boulevard, Suite 200
Colorado Springs, Colorado 80921

This book is not intended to replace the advice of a trained psychological professional. Readers are advised to consult a qualified professional regarding treatment. The author and publisher specifically disclaim liability, loss, or risk, personal or otherwise, which is incurred as a consequence, directly or indirectly, of the use or application of any of the contents of this book.

All Scripture quotations, unless otherwise indicated, are taken from The Holy Bible, English Standard Version, copyright © 2001 by Crossway Bibles, a division of Good News Publishers. Used by permission. All rights reserved. Scripture quotations marked (KJV) are taken from the King James Version. Scripture quotations marked (MSG) are taken from The Message by Eugene H. Peterson. Copyright © 1993, 1994, 1995, 1996, 2000, 2001, 2002. Used by permission of NavPress Publishing Group. All rights reserved. Scripture quotations marked (NLT) are taken from the Holy Bible, New Living Translation, copyright © 1996, 2004, 2007. Used by permission of Tyndale House Publishers Inc., Carol Stream, Illinois 60188. All rights reserved.

Italics in Scripture quotations reflect the author's added emphasis.

Details in some anecdotes and stories have been changed to protect the identities of the persons involved.

Trade Paperback ISBN 978-1-60142-738-0
eBook ISBN 978-1-60142-739-7

Cover design by Kelly L. Howard

Published in the United States by WaterBrook Multnomah, an imprint of the Crown Publishing Group, a division of Penguin Random House LLC, New York.

WaterBrook® and its deer colophon are registered trademarks of Penguin Random House LLC.

Library of Congress Cataloging-in-Publication Data
Wojo, Rachel.
    One more step : finding strength when you feel like giving up / Rachel Wojo.—First Edition.
        pages cm
    Includes bibliographical references.
    ISBN 978-1-60142-738-0—ISBN 978-1-60142-739-7 (electronic) 1. Christian women—Religious life. 2. Suffering—Religious aspects—Christianity. 3. Encouragement—Religious aspects—Christianity. I. Title.
    BV4527.W5675 2015
    248.8'43—dc23

                                        2015023682

Printed in the United States of America
2015—First Edition

10 9 8 7 6 5 4 3 2 1

Special Sales
Most WaterBrook Multnomah books are available at special quantity discounts when purchased in bulk by corporations, organizations, and special-interest groups. Custom imprinting or excerpting can also be done to fit special needs. For information, please e-mail SpecialMarkets @WaterBrookMultnomah.com or call 1-800-603-7051.

~ ~ ~

Mom,
You took me to the library every week,
bought books for me as gifts upon my request,
and fostered a love for reading and writing.
That was only the beginning.
Can't wait to see you again.

Contents

Let us not grow weary of doing good, for in due season we will reap, if we do not give up.

—Galatians 6:9

Permission to Ache Freely

That Christ hath regarded my helpless estate,
and hath shed his own blood for my soul.

—Horatio G. Spafford

Tension forced an ache into my entire body as I curled into a tight ball on the bed. Mounting circumstances seemed too much for my mind to continue functioning, and unfathomable stress choked every inch of my being. Every cell throbbed, pressing in my eyelids and numbing my lips.

I had stood at my mother's graveside three weeks ago. Shouldn't the overwhelming grief subside soon? How could sorrow envelop someone to the point of being unable to perform simple tasks? I used every ounce of strength I possessed merely to get out of bed. I felt panicked by everyday tasks of preparing for work and caring for my family.

The personal life storms I had endured for months relentlessly flooded my mind. On top of my mother's death, other difficult circumstances had crashed over me for the last fourteen months. I didn't think I would be able to continue to hold up; it was all too much.

No tears remained to trace their familiar path down my cheeks, but I sobbed on without them. Life hadn't always been this difficult.

As a child, I never experienced severe personal failure. I grew up in a wonderful Christian home, and my parents ensured that our family was faithful to church. I attended Christian school and then Christian college. And after I graduated, I completed the cycle of Christian education by teaching in a Christian school. My future husband was a "preacher boy," and when we married, the plan was that he would take a youth pastor position wherever God led.

Life as an adult offered a wonderful beginning, full of glorious hopes and beautiful dreams. But I soon discovered that no one is exempt from problems, and my perfect beginning didn't last long. Things changed drastically in a few short years. I found myself in a place I never dreamed I would be—divorced and a single mom of a child with special needs. Every day for months I felt as though I walked in a fog.

In the midst of my painful circumstances, I still had to maintain a house, care for my little girl, and work a full-time job. I had to figure out details, like how to pay for childcare and which facility could best care for my daughter while I was at work. We lived on a very tight budget, yet I still couldn't pay all the bills.

It seemed that people at church weren't quite sure how to handle my divorce, and shame cloaked my soul as I felt their disappointment. Maybe folks didn't know what to say to me at church, but I sensed that they gossiped behind my back. I chose to find a new church and even new friends. And I began to rethink my purpose in life and redefine my faith. I questioned what I was living for. What did God want to do with a divorced single mom of a child with special needs?

Three weeks after I said good-bye to my mom, I felt as if the world was spinning but I wasn't physically dizzy. Have you ever been there? When the storm in your heart transfers itself to your head and nothing in life makes sense? I know you have.

Every person on earth experiences difficult times at some point or another in this journey called life. Sometimes the difficulties simply add up. Two plus two equals four and before you can blink, a pile of problems results. Other times, the difficulties expand far faster than addition problems. Suddenly, the issues seem to multiply exponentially. Before you know it, the feeling of wanting to give up has saturated your spirit and you feel like you can't take even one more step. You have lost every ounce of strength in your mind, body, and spirit.

Whether it's unemployment, loss, unfulfilled dreams, marital issues, financial struggles, infertility, family heartaches, or disease, the list can go on and on. The issues often lead to the same feeling—wanting to quit. Stop trying. Stop pursuing. Stop everything.

No one begins a journey in hopes it will end before they get too far down the path. The roads of life don't begin with detour signs, and people don't start with the feeling of wanting to give up. Not one person sets goals because she wants to fail. The beginning of a journey usually appears to be streamlined. We calculate the route from point A to point B and draw plans to connect our dreams with real life. We want to finish strong, but circumstances creep in, people change, and negative feelings emerge.

I Thought No Crying Was Allowed

When I first began to experience extremely difficult life circumstances, like disaster, divorce, disease, and death, I started to read the book of Psalms on a regular basis. You may know that many of the psalms are songs of praise and adoration: *Praise the Lord. Praise ye the Lord. Praise him in the heavens; praise him in the heights . . .* These were the psalms I memorized in Christian school and church. They are good and holy and honorable. They resound with the goodness of God and his glory. The psalms give people a sense of joy and peace, right? Surely their inclusion in the Bible was intended to help us praise the Lord, and to think otherwise would be theologically unsound, am I right? Oh, I was so wrong about this.

In all my years of growing up in God's Word, I don't remember ever reading Psalm 88. This particular psalm certainly wasn't one on the Christian education memorization list. And I sure wish it would have been.

> O Lord, God of my salvation;
>> I cry out day and night before you.
> Let my prayer come before you;
>> incline your ear to my cry!
>
> For my soul is full of troubles,
>> and my life draws near to Sheol.
> I am counted among those who go down to the pit;
>> I am a man *who has no strength,*
> like one set loose among the dead,
>> like the slain that lie in the grave,
> like those whom you remember no more,
>> for they are cut off from your hand.
> You have put me in the depths of the pit,
>> in the regions dark and deep.
> Your wrath lies heavy upon me,
>> and you overwhelm me with all your waves. (verses 1–7)

Right in the middle of the book of Psalms, my soul awoke to a different tune than I had anticipated in this epic musical collection. That day was a new one for me, all because I discovered that the Bible actually contains a sad song. Not just any sad song, but a song that seemed as though I could have penned it. The entire melancholy psalm contained no praise, only heartache. The psalmist's expression leaked desperation and depression; he oozed sorrow over uncontrollable circumstances.

Could it be that God placed this sad song in the middle of the Bible to let people like me know that it's okay to ache with the sadness and hardness of this world? That it's good to let God know we're struggling and can't understand why the pit is so deep? That we don't have to pretend everything is perfect all the time and it's okay to express negative emotions?

As a child, I experienced difficulty in expressing myself, especially when things happened outside of my control. Melancholy was my middle name. When my passionate spirit once exhibited itself, one of my pastors declared, "Rachel, you're like the little girl with the little curl. When she was good, she was very good. And when she was bad, she was horrid." I never forgot his words because I didn't want to be horrid. I just didn't know how to express what I was feeling. Once I did begin to express any negative feelings, I felt that my expressions were frowned on. Psalm 88 seemed to be a psalm written just for me—the girl who desperately wanted to be good but often felt horrid, even with Jesus living in her heart.

This psalm echoed much of my heart's cry. *God, I need you. I need you to tell me why all these things are happening to me and why I have to go through these burdens. I feel like I'm in hell, Lord. Take me out of this crazy mind-set and wild circumstances.*

The First Step Out of the Pit

Psalm 88 beautifully informs us that God longs to listen to our sad songs. He wants to hear our hearts cry out to him, even when we don't understand his plan or are missing the lessons he wants to teach us. He loves to listen to our needs, and it's all right to tell him, *Yes, Lord, I'm overwhelmed. Help me, Jesus, please. Do you even remember me? Because all these situations I'm encountering are killing me. I need you, Jesus.* When we arrive at this point, we're in a good place.

Recognizing we want to give up is the first step toward realizing the pit we're in. Once we recognize that God wants to hear our cries, we can start to work our way through the feelings of despair. The psalmist continued to process his emotions:

> You have caused my companions to shun me;
>> you have made me a horror to them.
> I am shut in so that I cannot escape;
>> my eye grows dim through sorrow.
> Every day I call upon you, O LORD;
>> I spread out my hands to you.
> Do you work wonders for the dead?
>> Do the departed rise up to praise you?
> Is your steadfast love declared in the grave,
>> or your faithfulness in Abaddon?
> Are your wonders known in the darkness,
>> or your righteousness in the land of forgetfulness?
>
> But I, O LORD, cry to you;
>> in the morning my prayer comes before you. (verses 8–13)

The psalmist had lost friends because of his depressed state of mind. He couldn't see anything and he begged God to take him out of the dark. He'd lost the ability to see God's faithfulness and he'd forgotten how good God really is. He didn't know what else to do but pray.

Have you ached with the sadness of crushing life circumstances? Have your friends left you high and dry because they don't know how to cope with your pain? Have you felt that you can barely force the words through your mind even to talk to God? Besides losing friends, you feel like you don't know where God is either.

My heart aches for you; I can relate to that feeling. The psalmist felt this way too.

> O Lord, why do you cast my soul away?
>> Why do you hide your face from me?
> Afflicted and close to death from my youth up,
>> I suffer your terrors; I am helpless.
> Your wrath has swept over me;
>> your dreadful assaults destroy me.
> They surround me like a flood all day long;
>> they close in on me together.
> You have caused my beloved and my friend to shun me;
>> my companions have become darkness. (verses 14–18)

Perhaps you too have wondered, *God, why? Why do I have to live through all these problems? Why are you doing this to me? Everyone hates me; my spouse thinks I'm crazy and my friends have all ditched me. How can I see you through this darkness?* Isn't it interesting that this is where the sad song of Psalm 88 ends? The psalmist offered no resounding praise to the Lord for delivery from the pit. There was no hoopla or grand finale of joyful feelings over being restored. The psalmist didn't end with a glorious resolution to his emotional turmoil.

Psalm 88 is a beautiful gift to us—one that we both need and crave. God loves us so much that he gives us the permission to ache freely. What a gift! He's saying it's really okay to let him know about our bad days and the feelings we experience over horrible circumstances.

God would rather hear about your bad day than not hear from you at all. It's okay to tell him that we aren't loving life and that this current daily grind leaves us feeling unsatisfied and disheartened. He wants us to tell him when our hearts are heavy and hurting just as much as he wants us to tell him when we're happy and thankful. That's how much he loves us.

Choosing Prayer over Panic

In spite of all the negative emotion the psalmist expressed in his melancholy song of honesty, his word choices reveal positive points as well. In verse 1, he addressed God as the "God of my salvation." The psalmist knew God personally, but he was fighting a battle of will and emotion. I'm quite familiar with this battle and I'm sure you are too. It's the fight of what we choose to do with our feelings. We can't always control how we feel about an issue, but we can choose how we respond to those feelings. We can choose to channel the feelings in the right direction. This was the psalmist's challenge.

The psalmist also stated his cry was continuous, "day and night." The writer was a prayer warrior who believed in the power of continual honest expression before a holy God. He acknowledged that prayer was his lifeline.

What can we learn from his example? Prayer itself is a reminder of how good God is. The opportunity to communicate directly with the Creator of the universe is a gift of grace. God loves to hear our prayers, no matter our word choice. This psalm is proof. So when we experience feelings of desperation and we're tempted to plunge into despair, we must remember to pray before any other action.

Prayer trumps panic. Every. Time.

Not only was the psalmist panicked, but repetition indicates the depth of his despair. By the time we arrive at verse 9, the writer has repeated "every day I call upon you." He wasn't experiencing these issues for the first time. His battle had been ongoing. His lips expressed the same sorrow one more time, hoping for relief, though none was in sight.

In the same breath, the psalmist held his hands wide open, palms up, and remembered that he had surrendered everything. He'd given it all to the Lord; he wasn't holding tight to anything. And yet complaints and sorrow continued to pour from his soul for the remainder of the psalm.

Through the inclusion of this sad song in the middle of praise songs galore, I felt as though I had discovered a glorious character trait of God.

God understands human emotion because he created human emotion; you will never experience an emotion that he doesn't understand.

God understands our need to express feelings. He doesn't need me to wear a mood ring so he can determine what I'm feeling. He knows exactly when I feel like giving up. He knows exactly when you feel like giving up. God will not change if we are sad and depressed. He is forever the same and he loves us no matter the feelings we experience. He also understands how much we need someone to listen, and he is there for us, always the willing listener. He has promised never to leave us alone, and his promises never fail (see Deuteronomy 7:9).

It's More Than Okay to Cry

In spite of all the pain and loss of the "perfect" life, God uniquely and graciously brought Matthew into my life and we eventually married. Over the past fifteen years God has abundantly blessed us with a wonderful story of grace and redemption. Our blended family consists of each of our girls plus five more sweet children.

Only two months after Matt and I married, while we were still in the midst of adjusting to our new life together, my dear mom lost her battle with leukemia and went to heaven.

That day I described at the beginning of the chapter, when I could only lie on the bed and grieve, the bedroom door creaked open. Matt walked in the room and sat beside me. His words stumbled over each other as he felt my pain, and he spoke softly in his deep voice, "I don't know what to do to help you. But this helped me when I was in an extremely hard place." He rested his open Bible on the pillow beside me, and after holding me for a few minutes, he left the room.

He didn't tell me to stop crying. He didn't tell me I should be over the hurt by now. He gently let me know that he wanted to help but didn't know what to do. Mostly he gave me a huge gift: he pointed me to the One who invites us to pour out our hearts before him (see Psalm 62:8).

Life is messy and full of surprises. I know you know that. As you work your way through this book, you'll find that there's no judgment here for your hurting heart. In this first chapter, I want to give you the same gift God gives us through this beautiful psalm. The gift?

The permission to ache freely.

Finding strength begins with honesty with God. You don't have to sit high on the mountain of victory or even imagine you are sitting high on that mountain. I'm not going to ask you to dream of the finish line medal or think about how good it is going to feel once you get through the valley. We're not going to chat about lofty goals or unfathomable aspirations.

I've been through divorce. I've faced the death of my mama. I'm holding the hand of a special-needs child who suffers daily. I know what it's like to stare at disaster and feel desperation. There are no shortcuts. I found that I can best walk the path of life when I do it one step at a time. And that's what we're going to do together.

We are going to find the strength to take

one

more

step

when we feel like giving up.

⌒ ⌒ ⌒

Pillars of Truth to Lean On

At the end of each chapter, you will find pillars of truth for the journey. I'll share the Bible verses that I've depended on in order to make it one more step. You can use these verses to focus your heart and mind on the truth of God's Word and know that he is with you every step of the way. So lean on these verses to help you remember that God longs to hear you pray, regardless of how you feel.

- Hear my prayer, O LORD, and give ear to my cry; hold not your peace at my tears! (Psalm 39:12)
- Trust in him at all times, O people; pour out your heart before him; God is a refuge for us. (Psalm 62:8)
- I cry to you, O LORD; I say, "You are my refuge, my portion in the land of the living." (Psalm 142:5)
- The LORD is near to all who call on him, to all who call on him in truth. (Psalm 145:18)

Stepping Stone #1

Welcome to the first stepping stone of *One More Step*! Together we are going to take small steps at the end of each chapter to help us practically apply the material covered. You can use a blank journal of your own or download a free, beautiful *One More Step* printable companion journal. (Just go to http://rachelwojo.com/onemorestep.)

Recognizing you want to give up is the first step to finding true strength. Now that we recognize that the search for strength begins with God, pray and tell God everything on your heart. When you feel ready, challenge yourself by writing a prayer or letter to God, expressing all your frustrations and pain. Be completely open and honest. Congratulations! This stepping stone is your first prayer journal entry.

A Place for Hope

Whispering hope, oh, how welcome thy voice,
Making my heart in its sorrow rejoice.

—Septimus Winner

One day early in my first marriage, I woke up to the blaring 7:00 a.m. alarm, briefly wishing for a snooze button. The earlier-than-normal alarm meant that Sunday had arrived, so I rushed into the shower before the baby woke.

I never realized how much work it was to take a baby to church until I had one of my own. As a teenager, I'd worked in the church nursery at least on a monthly basis. All the moms seemed to have their acts together as they would smile and pass their babies to me, reassuring me that "everything is in the diaper bag." Who knew how much work it took to get to that point and make that proclamation? I was clueless until it was my turn to pack one for my own sweet baby.

Somehow this Sunday I managed to have my baby girl ready when it was time to leave for church, but my husband? He wasn't ready.

"Go on without me," he told me. "I'll be there shortly."

So I made my way to Sunday school, and he arrived in time for the worship service.

Before I knew it, Sunday arrived once more, and I hit the alarm, packed up my baby girl, and headed out to church without my husband. Only this week, he didn't show up for the service.

A few months went by, and one day as I drove to church, the blinding tears required me to pull my car over to the roadside. Choking back sobs, I realized that my Pollyanna hopes of serving the Lord in ministry were nowhere in sight. I rarely missed a church service, but my husband? He no longer attended.

When I fell in love with the man I thought would be pastoring a church someday, I hoped big hopes and dreamed big dreams. I could see myself serving the Lord in some ministry capacity, and I imagined it would be completely captivating and fulfilling. My thoughts of what God was going to do in our lives streamed wildly in my mind, accompanied by the desire to have a wonderful family. God had graciously given us the first baby of that dream.

Certain segments of life are imprinted on our minds forever. For me, one of those times is that day when I sat in the car on the side of the road, blinded by tears over my crumbling marriage. Another one of those times was two years later when I lay wide awake all night, realizing that my husband was in love with another woman. The pieces of the puzzle came together in the darkness, and I hated myself for taking so long to figure it out.

In spite of the great protective environment I experienced growing up, including attending church every week, often three times a week, sin had rudely interrupted my "perfect" life. Our marriage was under fire and I was completely unprepared. We attempted counseling. We separated. We "dated." We really tried for six months. But in the end, we could not resolve the issues and we divorced.

I was angry at God. How could this happen? Why would he allow my husband and this other woman to entertain a relationship? Overwhelming feelings of insecurity and emptiness flooded my heart and mind. Emotionally, I was scraping rock bottom. All I was capable of doing was getting through one more day.

I had placed so much hope in my husband. The kind that should not have rested in any person. When the marriage failed, my spirit weakened and I had zero strength. After the divorce, a rigorous soul searching ensued. There must be a better way to live. How could I have grown up in church, reading the Bible and praying, yet have no hope beyond making it through another day?

That serious soul searching unexpectedly revealed hard-core truth. You see, the raw bottom line uncovered that my faith was mostly a heritage. While I'm thankful for my family's wonderful, godly legacy, I didn't have a strong faith of my own. Oh, I trusted God to take me to heaven and I believed everything in the Bible. But most of my faith centered on to-do items on a checklist. I read the Bible because it was what I was supposed to do, and I prayed because it was the right thing. My prayers existed on a shallow basis; my faith was weak and vulnerable.

Have you ever experienced anger and hurt so deeply you can barely make it through the daily motions of existence? If you have, then you've never forgotten it. Maybe you are there right now, and you know from the experience that you need a hope you can stand on, not something that will fizzle out when you enter the hard spaces of life.

I was there. Living in that hard space no one wants to label: that feeling of wanting to give up.

Hope When We Feel Like Giving Up

When we feel like giving up and no hope seems to exist to heal our hurting hearts, searching for comfort is easy. During that awful time of attempting to survive through divorce, I sampled a few unhealthy choices, such as failing to eat properly, failing to exercise, and making friends with poor influences. I grasped at straws of hope in the form of self-reliance and self-image. After all, there's nothing like a new hairstyle to give you a boost of confidence, right? I tried independence and isolation from community as a means of protective hope. Although I never missed church services, I scooted in and out quickly so I could avoid conversation with anyone. On occasion, I sought approval from others in an attempt to find a strong place of hope, but this type of approval was short-lived. Before long, I realized no hope resulted from this type of behavior. To begin to hope requires us first to have a solid place for hope to rest.

Hope can be placed anywhere we choose, but the place we choose makes all the difference. Sometimes we believe we have landed on the "right" solution, only to find our discovery is anything *but* hopeful. We rest our confidence where it will not thrive, and our aching hearts experience negative emotional consequences.

When We Hope in Others

When we place our hope in people, we feel disappointed.

People let us down. As if I even need to say it, right? As much as we may like to think we are good judges of character, the truth is we are not mind readers. If we rest our hope in what we think humans might do or can do, then disappointment is sure to follow eventually, no matter who they are.

The problem with placing our hope in people is that people are . . . well. . .people. Inevitably, their hearts change, which changes their minds, which changes their actions. Soon we are left thinking, *I am so disappointed in so-and-so.* Considering human nature alone, people are not designed to hold our hope, especially concerning injured hearts.

When we set our hope in people, we miss the greatest source of hope. Not only do people change, but people make mistakes. We are all sinners and cannot avoid our humanity. Disappointment in others will leave scars of hopelessness that drill down far deeper than the surface. If we expect people to live up to the standards we have set for them, we set ourselves up for disappointment.

When We Hope in Things

So if we don't place our hope in people, where do we place it? Sometimes we place it in things. After all, objects aren't going to emotionally scar us. They don't hurt our feelings or say words that leave us wounded. Material possessions can seem like a great placeholder for hope, but there's one problem: satisfaction that stems from material possessions is temporary.

When we place our hope in things, we are distracted.

A new car can be a great temporary distraction when we no longer have to deal with the bad transmission on the old one. It's so easy to think, *If only I had a new house to replace this one, my family's situation would be so much better.* Or *If I could just land that new contract, we'd be okay.* Or *If the check would just come in the mail today, everything would improve.* But the truth is that material goods cannot provide hope. We may be able to rely on things temporarily with some success, but ultimately they will not fulfill or last.

Momentary satisfaction keeps us distracted from permanent hope, and in the end, causes more desperation. What do we do when the new kitchen appliances no longer gleam and the icemaker stops working? Or when the car has lost its new-car smell and the perfect house needs repairs? How do we handle it when the bank account dwindles or stocks fall? Focusing on things actually turns us away from true hope and moves us further from finding strength when we need it the most.

Sometimes chocolate dangles the promise of hope like nothing else, and I've been guilty of turning to a latte on occasion. Maybe you place hope in pizza and ice cream. (Come to think of it, I may or may not have used those as well.) I don't know what your "thing" is. Perhaps you feel this is an area in which you've learned your lesson. You recognize the familiar escapes, so you refuse to place your hope in things. Way to go! But maybe you have placed your hope somewhere else that results in negative emotional consequences. Perhaps without fully recognizing the fact, you've chosen to place your hope in yourself.

When We Hope in Ourselves

When we place our hope in ourselves, we can become devastated.

There are days when I feel like the little engine that could. My smokestack shoots higher into the air as my chest heaves with strength and power. The hope in myself puffs itself out like the cloud of pride it is. However, on the downside of the atrocious hill ahead lies a valley of toxic waste. The reality of my own weaknesses spews poisonous devastation over my spirit, anticipating the worst possible outcome in situations and destroying any ray of hope.

Self-confidence is important, but it can so easily develop into self-absorption or self-reliance or even arrogance. The truth is, we are only marginally more capable of making ourselves happy than someone else is of making us happy. We may think we know what we want and need, but too often this thought is a delusion built around our inability to see beyond immediate needs, desires, and circumstances.

When we place our hope in ourselves, we set ourselves up for failure in ways even more devastating than relying on external sources. Personal failure is most disappointing. I know I am much harder on myself than others. I have a more difficult time forgiving myself than I do others. Yes, I am a poor account holder for a commodity as precious as hope.

Our Ultimate Source of Hope

When we place our hope in Christ, we are delivered.

When we misplace hope, we open the door to feelings of giving up. So far we've learned that placing our hope in people results in disappointment. Can I get an amen? And we know that placing our hope in things causes distraction. Not to mention it's a temporary satisfaction. When we place our hope in ourselves, we wind up devastated. The only true resting place for hope is in Christ. Relying on the promises of God's Word and his love for us provides a firm foundation for our faith and trust.

Hope in people = Disappointed

Hope in things = Distracted

Hope in ourselves = Devastated

Hope in Christ = Delivered

Our hope is secure only when it is anchored in God and his Word—his love, his guidance, and his timing.

A Hopeless Woman

The hopeless woman in Luke 8:43–48 thought long and hard on her wish to break through the crowds and stand next to Jesus. She experienced menstrual issues, which kept her bleeding and unfit to socialize in her culture, according to the laws of the day. Can we stop for a second and think about this? Dealing with the bleeding problem itself must have been terrible, but to be a social outcast because of it? And furthermore, this problem had been going on not for days or weeks or months. This nameless woman had been dealing with the problem for twelve years. I can hardly wrap my brain around her endurance.

While each gospel tells her story, the book of Luke highlights it in a fresh way, revealing an important detail the others don't mention. "There was a woman who had had a discharge of blood for twelve years, and though *she had spent all her living on physicians,* she could not be healed by anyone" (verse 43).

Not only was this woman still suffering after twelve long years, but she had spent her last coin in an effort to find the right medical care.

Luke's mention of this detail clearly highlights how desperate the woman was. If only she could discover the antidote that would stop the bleeding.

We don't know if she saw Jesus heal others or if she had only heard stories of the miracles he had performed. We don't know if she wished for a moment to speak to him. Whatever the circumstances, she took the initiative to act on her hope. She believed that Jesus could heal her. If she could only get a little closer, if only the crowd wasn't so pressing . . .

Whatever her thoughts, she made her way to Jesus, one step at a time. When she was close enough, she reached out and simply touched his clothing. Her fingers didn't even make it to his skin, but with hope, by faith, they brushed the hem of his garment.

Instantly, the blood clotted. Her miracle came true.

However, in her ultimate moment of joy, fear struck her heart. He knew she had touched his clothing. "And Jesus said, 'Who was it that touched me?' When all denied it, Peter said, 'Master, the crowds surround you and are pressing in on you!'" (verse 45).

Do you think the woman was afraid to admit what she had done? She, who had been an outcast for years—how dare she touch the Son of God? Peter attempted to make logic of the situation. But of course, Jesus knew more had happened than Peter could fathom in the moment. And he said, "Someone touched me, for I perceive that power has gone out from me" (verse 46).

With trembling, the woman who bore the mark of "unclean" for more than a decade boldly stepped forward and declared her faith, as well as the result of it. She had to feel that no one could possibly understand. How could anyone really comprehend what she had endured for so many years?

But Jesus did. He said to her, "Daughter, your faith has made you well; go in peace" (verse 48).

The woman who suffered for so long received the gift of incomprehensible peace. Finally, after many years, the physical issue that marked her social status was gone. Permanently alleviated. I can only imagine the confidence she exuded after she heard those powerful three words: *Go in peace.*

The One Who Understands

Many times we lose our hope because we simply feel no one could possibly know what we are going through. After all, others may have experienced a similar loss, circumstance, or heartache, but we still believe, *They can't really understand what I am experiencing, because it's different.* The truth is no one can know for sure what we are feeling until we express it. Even then, perception and personal experience color how someone will perceive a situation.

Only Jesus comprehends every detail of what you are going through. Sent from heaven, Jesus arrived on earth as God in the flesh, the Almighty clothed in human skin. Not only did he take on physical form, but he also experienced emotions and limitations. God understands emotions not only because he created them but also because he experienced them.

Before he was crucified, Jesus knew the time was close. His anguish over future separation from God the Father tormented his soul. He cried and his sweat was like blood as it fell to the ground (see Luke 22:44). As he gathered his closest followers to pray in the garden of Gethsemane, his disappointment in their ability to stay awake and pray with him was evident in his question to them: "Why are you sleeping?" (verse 46).

Then the betrayal came: one of his own disciples personally delivered him to the enemy. The array of human emotion Jesus experienced because of Calvary is unfathomable to us.

The very character of God, his omniscience, promises us that he knows every detail of whatever we are going through, both the good and bad.

Our ability to keep going often begins with the decision of where to place our hope. Once we discover that Jesus is the only one who can hold our hope, we can begin to experience the strength he gives.

With the right resting place for hope, we can begin to think about taking one more step.

～ ～ ～

Pillars of Truth to Lean On

Let these Scriptures serve as reminders of the best place where we can rest our hope.

- Let your steadfast love, O LORD, be upon us, even as we hope in you. (Psalm 33:22)
- For God alone, O my soul, wait in silence, for my hope is from him. (Psalm 62:5)
- This I call to mind, and therefore I have hope: The steadfast love of the LORD never ceases; his mercies never come to an end; they are new every morning; great is your faithfulness. "The LORD is my portion," says my soul, "therefore I will hope in him." (Lamentations 3:21–24)
- Now may our Lord Jesus Christ himself, and God our Father, who loved us and gave us eternal comfort and good hope through grace, comfort your hearts and establish them in every good work and word. (2 Thessalonians 2:16–17)
- To this end we toil and strive, because we have our hope set on the living God, who is the Savior of all people, especially of those who believe. (1 Timothy 4:10)

Stepping Stone #2

We've learned that our hope is secure only when it rests in God and his Word. Leaving a large space at the top of a piece of paper, divide your sheet into three columns and label them with these headings: things, people, and myself. Then separately list the places in which you've allowed your hope to rest. You already know that mine might include something as small as chocolate or as large as a new house. Maybe your list will include the names of people or even your own talents. After writing out the list, cross out each one individually and write "Christ" across the top of the page. This stepping stone exercise will encourage your heart to remember that Christ is the only true hope.

three

Love: The Ultimate Pain Reliever

When nothing else could help, love lifted me.

—James Rowe

think I'm having a baby."

The previous night had provided little sleep as I tossed and turned. At one point, my back ached so much that I moved to the floor, hoping the firmness would provide some relief. Then I tried the rocking chair, only to find continued discomfort. I felt no hard pains, nothing stealing my breath, and I found myself wondering why I was even bothering to call the doctor. Yet somehow I pushed the words through my teeth as I made the phone call.

Shouldn't I have been able to identify true labor pains? Isn't labor easily recognizable as the spasms increase in severity and frequency? Doesn't every woman know this? Since this was my first maternity experience, I felt totally in the dark. Everything I felt was unanticipated this early, still three weeks short of my expected delivery date.

The doctor didn't sound convinced on the phone, but her advice was for me to head to the hospital. When I arrived at the emergency room, the triage nurse gave me "the look." The one that says, *There is no way this woman is having a baby today.*

However, before she could say any words, I mumbled, "I think my water broke." Truly, this all seemed foolish. Shouldn't I know if my water broke or not? The small popping noise I heard just after calling the doctor made me think that the sac of fluid protecting the baby had released, yet my clothing wasn't wet. I felt an undeniable twinge that something was going wrong, though I couldn't explain my feelings.

The nurse started wheeling me down the hall. Within a second, she gasped and said, "I think you're right, honey. Your water has broken!" I was trailing a stream of liquid. She whisked the wheelchair into a delivery room, and hospital staff appeared from nowhere. Somewhere in the background, I heard my doctor's name over the PA system, and the realization washed over me: *I am having a baby. Today!*

This thought brought a surge of happiness, but pain interrupted it. I was certain something wasn't right, yet as a new mama, I couldn't identify that "something." Instead of coming in a consistent pattern, the contractions occurred irregularly. I repeated phrases over and over to myself. *It will be okay. It's your first baby. Everything is fine.* But the words seemed to have the opposite effect. My panic level was rising, yet I couldn't describe the transformation taking place in my body. After multiple hours of contractions of varying degrees, the doctor inserted an internal monitor and attached it to the baby's head. I watched the numbers climb and then dip. What was going on?

Weariness collided with the anxiety of being a first-time mom. The pain grew in intensity, and fear gripped my heart that not only was there a problem with my labor's progress but also that something was wrong with my baby. I was growing more convinced by the minute that the contractions were harming the baby. I felt myself sliding into a state of shock as my blood pressure rose higher and higher.

Not long after the panic overwhelmed my mind, the doctor barged into the delivery room and barked out clear and concise instructions. "Your baby is not doing well. The heart rate is accelerating and then declining with each contraction, and the baby is in severe distress. We are taking you to surgery immediately to give your baby the best chance we can offer."

Seven minutes later, my baby girl was born via C-section. I'll never forget glancing up over the surgical curtain in joyful expectation of a healthy baby, only to see a purplish form. The nurse whisked her away for resuscitation. Terror seized my mind and body unlike anything I'd ever known.

My baby's Apgar score, the health rating assigned to babies, was 0 and her body was lifeless.

For what seemed like forever, the medical team worked on her until finally, miraculously, she breathed on her own.

Shivering on the operating table—as much from fear as temperature—as the doctor stapled me back together, I felt a sweet relief that could come only from heaven.

God delivered my baby girl that day in the operating room.

Just four days later Taylor came home from the hospital. As I snuggled her in my arms, tears fell from my cheeks to hers. I gently wiped them away as my heart swelled with thanks to God for allowing me to hold my precious baby who did not give up.

More than eighteen years later, I look back in awe at the birth of my sweet girl. As horrific as the agony was, remembering the anguish requires serious concentration. A faint memory of the worst pain is smothered by a love that overwhelmed my entire being from the first moment I saw her. **Love provides incredible pain relief.**

Have you ever encountered a heartache that took your breath away? Maybe it was due to a spouse who left you? Or a child who doesn't want to see you? Could it be a parent who can't recognize you anymore?

Smothered by the intensity, you don't define the pain as an ache. It shoots through every nerve in your body. Your mind is clouded by the brashness of its presence.

You seek relief but often overlook the greatest pain reliever. You can try to ignore it, medicate it, temporarily relieve it, numb it, treat it, or sedate it, but only accepting God's love can absolve pain.

Right now, you may feel as though you are holding your breath because the issues have overtaken you. They are so great that you can't see to the other side of them. Maybe you feel that you will never forget the depth of pain you've endured, whether seeing your baby lie in a casket or watching your long-loved parent slowly decline and lose strength. I don't know the hurts you've endured. But there's a woman in the Bible who knew overwhelming heartache, and we can glean a few principles from her.

Ruth's Love Story

Ruth became a widow after ten years of marriage in her homeland of Moab. We don't know exactly what happened to her husband, who was an Israelite, but I think we can understand that the death of a spouse is more than difficult. Not only did Ruth lose her husband, but she lost her father-in-law and brother-in-law also. Every male provider in the household was buried, and Ruth was left to make a living with her mother-in-law, Naomi, and sister-in-law, Orpah.

Can you grasp the depth of their sorrow, this triangle of widowed women? How much pain their hurting hearts must have endured.

After the death of her husband and two sons, Naomi caught word that the famine causing her family's initial move to Moab was over and food was now available in Israel. She decided to return home. As the trio began the trek to Bethlehem, however, Naomi determined that the best family solution was to leave her daughters-in-law in their own land of

Moab. As childless women, their hope for bearing children depended on finding new husbands. Fulfilling their cultural role would be a much simpler task if they returned to their families. As Naomi tried to think of someone who might be qualified to become a kinsman redeemer for her daughters-in-law, she came up short. She could not think of any relatives who would assume the marriage roles of her sons, as the laws dictated.

The three women stood together, emotions running high. As the older woman, Naomi freed the daughters from the bondage of caring for her and sent them back with her blessing. Her hope for each of them included finding a new husband. The Bible says, "Then she kissed them, and they lifted up their voices and wept" (Ruth 1:9).

Imagine the pivotal, life-changing decision these women had to make just as they were about to begin the journey together. Can you see them standing at the crossroads, weeping through the memories of better days and attempting to take the next step? Heartache had woven their hearts together, and the younger two women felt the connection too strong to leave their mother-in-law's side. They proclaimed their devotion and firmly fought the elder woman's words. No way were they going to leave their dear mother-in-law without any family at all. Hadn't she endured enough sorrow through the loss of her husband and sons?

But Naomi began to state the logic behind her advice. "Girls, I'm too old to remarry and I have no more sons for you to marry. There is no reason for you to stay with me and bear the same burden that I am—that of losing your entire inheritance and family tree." And then Naomi declared her bitterness at God for the situation.

> But Naomi said, "Turn back, my daughters; why will you go with me? Have I yet sons in my womb that they may become your husbands? Turn back, my daughters; go your way, for I am too

old to have a husband. If I should say I have hope, even if I should have a husband this night and should bear sons, would you therefore wait till they were grown? Would you therefore refrain from marrying? No, my daughters, for it is exceedingly bitter to me for your sake that the hand of the LORD has gone out against me. (verses 11–13)

This round of declaration resulted in another round of emotional torrent and weeping.

When I read this account, the bond of sorrow between these women captured my attention and I tried to put myself in their places. Twice in these few verses, they wept and clung to one another. Their emotions ran soul deep.

But as with all decisions, at some point they had to stop crying and step forward in the journey. With Naomi begging the girls to move on with their lives, Orpah decided to follow her advice, so she headed back to her own people. But Ruth? She couldn't bring herself to the same decision, and she said so with words that have been echoed for centuries.

Do not urge me to leave you or to return from following you. For where you go I will go, and where you lodge I will lodge. Your people shall be my people, and your God my God. Where you die I will die, and there will I be buried. May the LORD do so to me and more also if anything but death parts me from you. (verses 16–17)

In short, she said, "Over my dead body" (Wojo paraphrase). This girl was serious!

I wonder if through this whole experience, Naomi ever asked God why these things had happened to her. Why did he take her husband? Why did he take her sons? Why did he leave her childless? And why did all of these circumstances happen to *her*? Couldn't someone else lose her entire family? Couldn't someone else endure hardship in a foreign country? What was God thinking?

While Naomi asked God why, Ruth made a commitment. We don't know Ruth's line of reasoning; we're not privy to her thoughts before she made her bold address. We don't know if or how long she deliberated. One thing birthed her direct words of determination: Ruth's hope had grown roots of love. Love is the reason she chose to stay with Naomi.

Instead of allowing painful life circumstances to infuse weakness in her relationship with Naomi, Ruth used the situation to empower herself and others. Her personal feelings of pain became fuel to unite their hearts rather than separate them.

Would Ruth's devotion to Naomi have been so strong had they not endured such heartache together? Perhaps Ruth feared for Naomi's life. Maybe she saw her mother-in-law sinking into depression and so she refused to walk away from her. Perhaps she was worried about Naomi's physical needs and whether or not she would have food and shelter. Whatever the reason, Ruth loved her mother-in-law and gave her every ounce of commitment she possessed.

Standing at this crossroads moment, Ruth could have made a completely different choice. But she chose to continue loving Naomi, and she proved her love by refusing to leave Naomi alone.

I know you've experienced turning point decisions like Ruth's. While I don't know the decision you made, whether to love and be loved or withdraw and lose touch, Ruth shows us that determining to love was a pivotal step in her journey. Choosing to give and receive love freely brought unbelievable pain relief and strength to her heart.

Our Love Story

It's so easy to be confused in how we think about hope and love. If we choose to place our hope in Christ, then we experience his love. But many times we feel like giving up because we forget how much God really loves us. When negative emotions overtake our minds and hearts, we lose focus on the love of God.

In the midst of my marital struggle, I lost sight of God's love. I forgot how much he loves me and that he can use anything for my good. My focus strayed from his hope and love, and I looked to others to fulfill both physical and emotional needs. Oh, I still attended church and went through the motions of what seemed to be right. But I had strayed away from loving God personally and intimately. I never opened my Bible to read his words of love to me. And my prayers consisted of requests and demands. God and I were barely acquaintances and certainly not friends. I even gave my attention to worldly people and sinful pleasures, meanwhile completely forgetting just how much God really loves me.

We fall in love, trip over it, stumble upon it. But God? His path is love because *he* is love.

John reminds us of God's love when he states: "Beloved, let us love one another, for love is from God, and whoever loves has been born of God and knows God. Anyone who does not love does not know God, because God is love" (1 John 4:7–8).

Maybe you've never fully recognized who God is. Perhaps today is the first day you are hearing that God loves you so much that he sent his Son to die on the cross for the sin of the entire world—including mine and yours (see John 3:16). His love is a gift to us and we don't need to do anything to earn his forgiveness. We simply believe that his death on the cross was a love gift to us and we ask for forgiveness of our sin.

You could be one who knows the love of God and has already accepted it, but you've experienced circumstances that have caused you to stop receiving his love. When you choose not to spend time talking to him and reading his love letter, it can be easy to forget how much he really loves you. Even when you do spend time with God, you may still feel distant from him.

How so?

Let's pretend for a moment that I'm angry at my husband. Now, I love him to the moon and back and more, but in a temporary moment of anger, I'm upset with him for some crazy reason. He comes home from work and unloads his keys and work bag. Then he comes to the kitchen sink and wraps his arms around my waist. Quietly he whispers in my ear, "Hey, how was your day?" And I let him do all of this, but I don't return his affection or attention. I say simply, "It was okay," then avoid eye contact and move from the sink to the stove.

Did I speak to him? Yes. Did I listen to him? Yes. But did I give him my attention and affection? No. Did I look him in the eye and say, "It was good. Thanks for asking. How are you?" No.

Sometimes the Hope of the World wraps his arms around us and asks us about our day, and we say, "It was okay." We don't return his affection or attention; we avoid eye contact and move on to the next thing. One overwhelming attribute of God's love is that it never fails. He never gives up on us. His love never runs out on me. Or you. You see, God wants our love in return, but he doesn't force it. He gives us the privilege to choose.

Maybe you're asking, "How do you know?"

When my ex-husband chose another woman over me, I made some poor choices. I never missed church once I realized marital bliss had disappeared. But I was angry and bitter. I was upset at God for allowing this woman to see my ex-husband and for my ex-husband to continue to see her. And I felt that God was to blame. After all, couldn't he have stopped them from continuing their relationship? And if he hadn't let me grow up in the wonderful, protective environment I'd always known, then maybe I wouldn't have been so naive.

So I stood at the kitchen sink of my life, and when God came and wrapped his arms around me, gently whispering, "How was your day?" I replied, "It was okay." Then I moved on to the daily demands of being a single mom. The job, the house, the car, the child. I didn't want to give him eye contact because wasn't it his fault I was in the situation? Oh, my heart missed his tenderness, but I refused to be close to the God I loved, so I held him at a distance.

However, God is love. He doesn't just do it, speak it, act it. He *is* it (see 1 John 4:16). When I pushed him to arm's length and further, he wooed me back. His Spirit prompted me to think of a verse I had memorized as a child, and I knew that he was speaking to my heart. An old friend sent me a kind, compassionate letter, and I knew God was whispering, *I still care for you as much as ever.* I knew that many people, especially my parents, were praying for me. Gradually I listened to his voice speak into my life more and more. His word and the actions of Christians he placed in my life spoke love into my heart. Though my decision took longer than Ruth's, eventually I chose the way of love and committed myself to him anew. The more I recognized his love for me, the more I began to receive it. The more I received it, the more pain relief I experienced. I realized that God's love is bigger than my pain, and this realization provided healing to my hurting heart.

God desires a personal relationship with me—not a religious experience for me.

Can you hear him whispering to your heart? Maybe through the words of a friend who invited you to church or Bible study. Perhaps through a social media blurb or a phone call from your concerned parent.

Did you think that the pastor must have been following you all week when his sermon seemed to be exactly what you needed? While reading this chapter, did the thought come to mind, *That's me. How did she know?* All these are whispers of God's love, and love is God's prescription for pain.

～ ～ ～

Pillars of Truth to Lean On

Use these Scriptures every day as love promises to remind you of just how much God loves you personally.

- By day the LORD commands his steadfast love, and at night his song is with me, a prayer to the God of my life. (Psalm 42:8)
- Nor height nor depth, nor anything else in all creation, will be able to separate us from the love of God in Christ Jesus our Lord. (Romans 8:39)
- See what kind of love the Father has given to us, that we should be called children of God. (1 John 3:1)
- In this the love of God was made manifest among us, that God sent his only Son into the world, so that we might live through him. (1 John 4:9)
- There is no fear in love, but perfect love casts out fear. For fear has to do with punishment, and whoever fears has not been perfected in love. (1 John 4:18)
- We love because he first loved us. (1 John 4:19)

Stepping Stone #3

Choose one verse from the list above that relays God's love to you in a personal way. Write it on an index card or use the printable *One More Step* journal (download it at the URL link on page 12) and copy it five times. Read this verse aloud for thirty days and memorize it as a stepping stone to remember how much God loves you.

four

The Buried Treasure of Trusting God

> Just from Jesus simply taking life and rest, and
> joy and peace.
>
> **—Louisa M. R. Stead**

t was one of those moments I wish happened anywhere other than the church building. If I wasn't in church, well, I might have suffered less guilt over my longing to slap the woman across the face. And more than that, I wouldn't have the scene permanently burned in my memory as a "church" moment—you know, the ones that affect your view of church people and, ultimately, all Christians.

Before that day, I knew my sweet girl, Taylor, was developing slowly for her age, and the doctors had assured me time and time again that this issue was most likely due to her lack of oxygen at birth. I had no way to know how long her infant brain had gone without oxygen, and though the doctors didn't give any indication that she would suffer permanent damage, her overall behavior wasn't completely age appropriate. I carried this knowledge with me like an overstuffed Samsonite, and the weight of it pressed on my heart. But I tried my best to believe that what the doctors said was true—after all, they are the professionals; how much knowledge could a first-time mama possess in comparison to their vast years of education?

Though Taylor's developmental progress was delayed, by age three, she'd hit most of her milestones. She had experienced many ups and downs with gastrointestinal issues, but all in all, we were happy with her rate of progress. Though she could not say many words, she understood and followed one-step instructions. She could feed herself, drink from a cup, and had definitely mastered undressing herself.

Taylor was such a happy child; rarely did she cry. Her smile radiated through halls and across malls. Even when I thought she might not be feeling well, she would hum little tunes and clap her hands for joy. Her beautiful light brown hair bounced, and I so enjoyed weaving it into french braids or pulling it up in two pigtails.

One week, after the church services were over, I went to the preschool wing to pick her up. Often her bubbly demeanor attracted attention, and the teachers would usually greet me with a big smile and comment on Taylor's joy. But this week, a teacher who had watched Taylor during many other church services called for her and then approached me, looking serious. I was surprised when, somewhat hesitantly, she pulled her glasses down over the bridge of her nose and peered at me over the rims.

In a hushed yet harsh tone, she said, "Do you ever notice Taylor doesn't act normal for her age?"

I gulped hard. "I realize she has some delays."

At which she shook her head slightly, as if I were in denial. "Don't you want to help your child?"

I didn't know how to respond. So I called for Taylor and quickly moved around the line of parents who had gathered behind me.

Once Taylor was buckled into her car seat and we were ready to leave, I could no longer hold back the tears. They streamed down my cheeks.

I wanted to scream at that woman, "Of course I want to help my child! How could you ask such a question?" But it was not in my nature to lash out at the inconsiderate frankness of others. No, it was much more my style to determine that "we" would show her. At that moment I made a promise to myself and Taylor. I would always defend her and make sure she had everything she ever needed for her success.

While the Sunday school teacher seemed to feel I was in denial over Taylor's delayed development, the opposite was true. Each day since bringing her home from the hospital, Taylor fought small battles of all types— and I did my best to help her. Keeping milk in her little tummy had been a challenge; she easily threw up right after drinking an entire bottle. Feeding her was a meticulous and scientific job. Soy formula was the only type she could digest, and I had to burp her after every two ounces. The doctors diagnosed her with esophageal reflux and gastroparesis—fancy words that meant her throat and stomach muscles didn't function properly.

Crawling didn't happen as with many children, but the medical professionals felt this delay was okay. Pulling herself up to stand occurred at an age-appropriate mark, and so did walking, though she seemed clumsy. She was busy and active but had difficulty following detailed requests. I knew her speech was delayed for a three-year-old, and county preschool evaluation tests revealed that she needed to begin speech therapy immediately. Still, each specialist would reiterate that, because of Taylor's lack of oxygen at birth, it would be years before they could predict her brain's development capability. So much growth happens from ages two to four that the doctors held a "wait and see" approach to her symptoms, while encouraging therapy.

A few months had passed since that teacher asked me if I wanted to help my child. The sting of her question had pierced my heart in such a way that I didn't trust anyone to care properly for Taylor. I kept watch over her every move and showed up to visit her in preschool and church at unexpected times. Things seemed to be going well: she could feed herself, and her speech was developing nicely. At age three, yes, she was delayed, mostly in speech, but her digestive issues had improved, and I felt hopeful.

One day, the two of us prepared to leave our condo and I asked Taylor to put on her socks. She looked up at me in acknowledgment, and I continued with my own preparations. After a couple of minutes, I looked down to see that she had not put her socks on her feet. So I asked her again. After all, she had been doing this for some time and I knew she could do it herself. Once again, I moved on. A couple of minutes later, I returned to find Taylor sitting in the same spot with a confused look on her face. For a split second I was upset and thought she was deliberately disobeying me, but when I looked into her eyes and watched her hands fumbling with the socks, I realized, *She doesn't remember how to put her socks on.*

The fears I had shoved off since her traumatic birth flooded my mind. Something more was wrong than a developmental delay due to oxygen deprivation at birth. She had lost a skill.

I thought I was trusting God. I never missed church and I read my Bible on a regular basis. I prayed every day and thought I was walking the right path. Even though I had chosen a few wrong friends after the divorce, I quickly broke those ties when it was evident they were not interested in living for God.

What does all this have to do with Taylor not being able to put her socks on? My mama instinct knew that whatever had caused Taylor to lose a skill she had already learned was way worse than the doctors initially believed. Trusting God was about to get real.

Out of Control

You've been there, haven't you? Those situations where trusting God was harder and bigger than you ever thought possible. When I was thinking about the things that often cause frustration in the trusting department, this list came to my mind:

- the weather
- the behavior of others
- the words of others
- material things that break, like the car, dishwasher, washer, dryer
- accidents
- health problems and sickness
- death

Each of these items has one thing in common: they are totally out of our control. We certainly can't keep a tornado from destroying our home. We can't prevent our mother-in-law from rearranging our cabinets. We surely can't keep the gossip from flowing out of Aunt Susie's mouth. The refrigerator isn't going to last forever. And inevitably, someone is going to break a leg. People get sick, and at some point, everyone dies.

The feeling of being out of control results in indescribable frustration. Frustration in coping with issues and handling situations we can't change is often the reason we feel like giving up. We begin statements with *I wish I could . . . If only . . . Why?* And when the frustration peaks, boldly we unveil the real question: *How can I find the strength to trust God when it seems that things are completely out of control?*

The One in Control

In Genesis 14–15, we find the story of a people who felt like things were out of control. Their journey of trusting God is one worth following.

After four hundred years of slavery in Egypt, the children of Israel, under Moses's leadership, began their path to freedom (see 15:13). Can you imagine the excitement? After all the years of being controlled by the taskmasters, the Israelite nation would finally be in control of themselves. The workday was no longer dictated to them. Suffering backs could heal from the torture of whips and cat-o'-nine-tails. A dim hope for the next generation gleamed in the eyes of parents.

Until they reached the Red Sea. How quickly the glimmer of hope dissipated as the rush of the Egyptian horses and chariots grew louder and millions of eyes stared at the huge body of water barring liberty. After encountering circumstances beyond their control for so many years, the children of Israel blamed Moses. They wished they were back in Egypt where at least they could have been buried in graves rather than dying in the wilderness (see Exodus 14:11).

But God had a bigger and better plan—a great reminder for us today. God's plan was to part the Red Sea and give his people the opportunity to walk across on dry land to the other side. The second part of his plan included destroying their Egyptian enemies and allowing the Israelites to see who was truly in control of their situation.

As I studied the story's details in Exodus 14, I discovered something I'd never noticed before: an angel of God had led the way for the children of Israel from the time they left Egypt.

> The angel of God who was going before the host of Israel moved
> and went behind them, and the pillar of cloud moved from before
> them and stood behind them, coming between the host of Egypt
> and the host of Israel. And there was the cloud and the darkness.
> And it lit up the night without one coming near the other all
> night. (verses 19–20)

The only thing separating the Egyptian armies and the children of Israel was a layer of cloud and darkness; the angel of God prevented them from crossing paths the entire night.

Why had I never noticed this before, this fact that they spent an entire night camping right next to one another? The Israelites certainly made their feelings clear about wishing they could give up on God's plan and go back to Egypt. What if they had given up and acted on those feelings? If they had known how close they were camped to the Egyptians, they would have been terrified.

The next morning, the Egyptians chased the Israelites to the Red Sea, where God provided an unlikely escape straight through it. **When things seem out of control, God is always in control.**

No record exists of the Red Sea being parted prior to the children of Israel walking on dry land that miraculous day. No, only one time did God work a miracle in this manner. I wonder what it was like to be the first person to step on the dry sea bed, especially as the wall of water stood beside them.

When there's nothing left to work with from a human perspective, God says, *No problem. I made humans from dust. In fact, I spoke the world into existence. I've got everything under control.*

As the Creator of the universe, God governs every molecule, every atom, and every cell. If he orders the smallest details of creation, why would the big picture of the universe be any different?

The children of Israel did not fully trust God's will; they wanted to turn back to captivity before they had even a small taste of independence. They actually thought their strategy of continuing as prisoners in Egypt was better than God's plan of total freedom.

Have you ever felt sure that your idea was a good one, maybe even a great one? And when God intervened with your plan, you grew so frustrated that things were out of order? And when things seemed out of hand, you wanted to be in control, right?

I experienced this when I wound up a divorced, single mama. Things were definitely outside of my expectations. I was trying my best to get all the circumstances under control, but the more I tried, the crazier things seemed to get. I'm thankful that God's plan was enormously larger than mine. He introduced a little piece of it in a unique manner.

Surrendering to God's Control

Back in the dark Internet ages, when social media was a futuristic thought blip and e-mail was fascinating, I came home from church one morning, totally amazed at what I had heard. No, it wasn't a deeply spiritual thought from the sermon or a Bible verse I'd never before read. I had overheard a discussion I couldn't believe, and I just had to check it out.

Could there really be a Christian Internet dating service?

I could hardly contain my curiosity when I searched for "Christian matchmaker" on my web browser. Who in their right mind signs up for an online dating service? Aren't people so crazy nowadays?

Sure enough, Christian online dating services existed! After going through marital separation and divorce, there was no way I was ready to date anyone. I'd made enough stupid judgment mistakes and I certainly had no intention of continuing this decision pattern. I had turned my back on the bad decisions I'd made and determined to continue on a straight path. But something compelled me to just check it out. I couldn't pinpoint it at the time, whether sheer curiosity or a tinge of loneliness, but whatever it was, I followed through.

In order to see anyone's profile, I had to register for a free ten-day trial and complete my own profile. Ugh. I just wanted to see what in the world people might put on there. I finally convinced myself: *Okay, I'll sign up for a free trial. What's it going to hurt?*

Upon completing the shortest profile ever, without even uploading a picture, I paused and then clicked SUBMIT. Watching the screen carefully, I had no idea what was going to happen, but the system flashed CHECK-ING COMPATIBILITY.

Meanwhile, I said a quick prayer: *Lord, I don't know about this, but it's all yours. I'm all yours.*

And then a list of names came up on the screen. The top one said, "Your top profile match is 52 percent."

So I clicked on it and Matthew's photo appeared. If the guy had just been on the dull side of masculinity, I would have found it easy to laugh and move on. But tall, dark, handsome, *and* matching 52 percent? I had always loved the name Matthew, and I felt compelled to read through his profile. Our family and church backgrounds were similar. I grew up in a family of nine children; he grew up in a family of five children. Our denominational backgrounds were the same. Both of us had attended Christian school and college.

Then I arrived at the testimonial portion of the profile. Good grief, this guy wrote a book.

Why would someone put all this information on a dating service if he wasn't serious? I wondered.

We had both experienced a failed marriage, but it was obvious that, like me, he was looking forward to God's plans for his future. The more I read, the more interested I became. Especially when he stated that his goals were to grow daily in his faith, raise his daughter to serve God, and continue to be active in the music ministry at his church. Hmmm. Sounded so similar to what I had just written in my journal a few days earlier! I could hardly believe it, but I felt as though God wanted me to write to this man. I could hear the Lord whispering to my heart that this match was not a coincidence.

So I wrote a short paragraph introducing myself to Matt and letting him know that I read his testimony. I didn't tell him in the e-mail, but the raw description of his personal prodigal son journey drew him to my heart.

He responded soon after, and a courtship was born. Only one month after I sent the initial e-mail, we met at the zoo to spend a day together with each of our girls. Immediately I had total peace that God brought Matt and me, as well as our girls, together.

One silly little e-mail sparked a love that only God could bless into fifteen-plus years of marriage, a beautifully blended family, and five children together, for a total of seven kids. God, in his providence, initiated a plan through that little e-mail. If I had known in advance that it was to use a dating service to join two lives and reclaim their stories for him, I'm not sure I would have believed it. But it's part of an enormous plan he wants to work in every life on the planet, a plan called "redemption."

Redemption is God transforming crazy circumstances into beautiful blessings. You see, God loves us so much that when he sent Jesus to die on the cross for us, he was buying back, "redeeming," his people. This means that not only can we trust him to save us and take us to heaven, but we can rely on him to give us a new story, even after we've made a mess of our lives.

In my case, he brought healing to my wounds and restored my trust in him, preparing my heart to risk unity with Matt's.

One of the really cool things God did through this unity of hearts was to use Matt to take me to a church where I would begin to understand the love of God even more. Yes, I had asked Jesus to be my personal Savior at a young age. Yes, I grew up in a wonderful Christian home. But much of following Christ up to this point had been a list of dos and don'ts. Through studying God's Word, praying, and being faithful to God's house, I began to whisper back to the Lord when he wrapped his arms around me, and I started to experience more and more of God's love and his beautiful plan of redemption. I began to trust him more.

Oh, how he wants to redeem you—all of you. Your hurts. Your failures. Your pain. But you have to be willing to accept his marvelous plan and to trust that he is who he says he is. You have to believe his promises— that he will do what he says he will do. You have to believe that the whisper of the Holy Spirit to your heart is real. That God is alive and at work in your life, even though you can't see him. That he is everywhere and everything, but you cannot touch him. That by faith, you have trusted him for salvation, and by faith, you believe that he is leading you through life.

Trusting God means you believe God is who he says he is and that he will do what he says he will do.

Your story may not include an online dating service. (You may be saying, "No, and thank you, Jesus." It's okay; I get it.) But you have your own set of crazy circumstances for which you need to trust God. Maybe you're like my friend who is in his fifties and who, after two divorces, is ready to embrace God's best in his life, hoping that includes a wife. Maybe you're like my friend whose sweet child was rushed to heaven before she had the opportunity to see the beauty of life. Perhaps your crazy circumstances include a teenager addicted to drugs or a parent entering the first stages of Alzheimer's. Our circumstances will change again and again. But God? He never changes.

His Word never changes and he is worthy of our trust.

Are you ready to tell him you believe that today?

～ ～ ～

Pillars of Truth to Lean On

Enjoy this list of some of my favorite verses for trusting God in tough times.

- He will hide me in his shelter in the day of trouble; he will conceal me under the cover of his tent; he will lift me high upon a rock. (Psalm 27:5)
- Commit your way to the LORD; trust in him, and he will act. (Psalm 37:5)
- In the day of my trouble I call upon you, for you answer me. (Psalm 86:7)
- Trust in the LORD with all your heart, and do not lean on your own understanding. In all your ways acknowledge him, and he will make straight your paths. (Proverbs 3:5–6)
- Every word of God proves true; he is a shield to those who take refuge in him. (Proverbs 30:5)
- Trust in the LORD forever, for the LORD GOD is an everlasting rock. (Isaiah 26:4)

Stepping Stone #4

Realizing that God's plan is always more incredible than we can imagine, write out three to five areas of your life where you know you need to trust God. (See the *One More Step* journal at rachelwojo.com.) Then talk to God about each of these areas, surrendering every facet and detail to his divine knowledge and wisdom. Now write out your prayer in your *One More Step* journal. Compare this entry to your first prayer journal entry from Stepping Stone #1 and celebrate the progress you've made in giving God control!

five

Gifts in the Desert

Let Thy goodness, like a fetter, bind my
wandering heart to Thee.

—Robert Robinson

decided it was high time to stop listening to doctors. When Taylor
couldn't put on her own socks, my instinct confirmed the need for medical due diligence and Mama Bear mode kicked in. There was something
more to her developmental disabilities than the standard label of "oxygen
deprivation at birth," and I was finished listening to their vague opinions.
Medical professionals were about to take a turn listening to me, whether
they liked it or not.

I could hardly believe my ears at the first appointment with a new
pediatrician. After listening to my explanation, unlike the twenty-some
doctors before him, this doctor looked into my eyes and spoke frankly.

"I don't know what is wrong with your daughter. But I am going to
send you to someone who can figure it out."

Did he really just say he didn't know? I decided any doctor with
this kind of integrity deserved to be in his profession. Not only was
he an honest man, but he actually followed through on his word. The
next day his office called me with a scheduled appointment to see a

developmental-delay specialist. Having a scheduled specialist appointment alone was an answer to prayer.

We had to wait six months in order to see the specialist. Finally the day arrived, and as we sat in the exam room and waited for her to enter, I hoped for an answer that would move us forward. I didn't know what to expect, and questions swirled through my mind. Would the doctor listen to the issues? Would she really be able to diagnose the problem? Would she have any treatment options?

Though it seemed forever, it wasn't long before the doctor entered the exam room. She was kind and spoke gently. She was not immune to Taylor's infectious joy, and soon the two of them were interacting and enjoying a color-matching game. She asked many questions of us, such as, What happened at her birth? Who does she look like? At what age did she learn to walk?

I could hardly believe she spent two hours in conversation and observation. Two hours! So many doctors Taylor had seen just pushed us through the standard protocol. This specialist's interest felt incredibly comforting and hopeful. As a mom who refused to allow professional opinions to supersede her own observations, I was encouraged simply by the doctor's willingness to listen.

Just four days later, we received a four-page report from the specialist. On the last page, she listed twelve diagnoses she wished to rule out. I was both elated and frightened at the list. I was elated for possible explanations and frightened of potential truth. That night after Taylor went to bed and Matt headed to third shift, I began to Google each diagnosis. One by one I read lists of symptoms, but none seemed to match all of Taylor's symptoms.

Methodically, I researched my way down the list until I reached the description and symptoms for mucopolysaccharidosis, known as MPS. I had never heard of the disease, but then, neither had I heard of any on the list. As I researched, I learned that the normal body uses enzymes to break down and recycle molecules, but with MPS, certain enzymes are missing or insufficient. Because the molecules are not properly broken down, they get stored in the body and distort, as well as eventually stop, normal processes. Children are not typically diagnosed until age three or later because doctors must be intuitive enough to recognize that something serious is wrong and request urine and blood tests to confirm diagnosis.

Often children are extremely active and restless, with very difficult behaviors. This symptom fit Taylor. There was no doubt that she was a busy child. I also read that some children sleep very little at night. That too was Taylor. I felt like I hadn't slept since the sweet girl was born, trying to keep an eye on her to make sure she didn't injure herself.

I combed through as many articles about MPS as I could find, searching and reading every piece of information I could on this rare neurologically degenerative disorder. The facts were overwhelming. Every article pointed to the same outcome: there was no cure or treatment for the disease, and the average lifespan approximated ten to fifteen years.

The more I read, the more anxious I became. The symptoms of MPS were an exact match to my sweet girl's problems since birth. My mother's heart knew that Taylor had MPS.

The waiting was over; I had the answer.

It just wasn't the answer I was looking for.

Where Are We Going?

Taylor was four years old when she was diagnosed with MPS, and she was ever so full of life. She didn't walk; she ran everywhere. Her hyperactivity created daily safety challenges. She was completely uninhibited by heights and had no sense of danger, like touching hot stoves or rushing out around moving cars. Her verbal skills were delayed for her age, but highly appreciated for her disease. She could sing in perfect pitch and knew the words to many songs—one of her most beautiful attributes was her singing voice.

She creatively used words to express herself, even when she couldn't find the right ones. Her own little vocabulary grew to include words and phrases that my husband and I still fondly use today, such as:

Te'bo'te meant "It's time to brush teeth."

Thank you welcome was truly an innovative way to save time by combining "Thank you" and "You're welcome."

Po'torn (popcorn) and *iteam* (ice cream) were favorite family snacks.

Our small family of four, including Matt, Tiffany (my stepdaughter), Taylor, and me, would travel regularly to visit out-of-town family members. Taylor could spot a McDonald's as though she possessed radar for it. She loved to order her Happy Meal with a "cheesehammer, fin fie, and pop." She also liked to repeat phrases, and whenever we traveled, she would ask one question over and over: "Where we goin'? Where we goin'?"

One of us would answer, "We're going home, TayTay" (or wherever we were going), only to have her ask again within three or four minutes: "Where we goin'? Where we goin'?"

It was the same question I was asking.

"God, where *are* we going?"

Desert, Not to Be Confused with Dessert

Taylor's inability to put on her socks was a sign of things to come. She would not be able to talk. She would probably never be potty trained for even a short time. Eventually every skill she possessed would be lost.

We had moved from the wilderness of not understanding what was wrong with our sweet Taylor to the desert of a terminal lysosomal storage disorder with an average lifespan of ten to fifteen years. As we stared at this unfamiliar disease, the medical definitions of no treatment and no cure appeared before us as an unending desert journey.

There are times when it seems you simply move from one desert to another. Do you recognize that dry place where nothing is happening and it seems that time is standing still as you wait for God? It's hot. You're thirsty. The heat pushes you to the brink of exhaustion. And not only is the waiting difficult, but everything in life seems to move continuously but without making true progress. You feel as though you are stuck, and you just keep thinking, *God, where in the world are we going?*

If you think about it, this feeling mirrors the children of Israel, our example from the last chapter. We left them staring back at the Red Sea after it had swallowed up an entire Egyptian army. Let's take a peek at where they wound up next.

> Israel saw the great power that the LORD used against the
> Egyptians, so the people feared the LORD, and they believed
> in the LORD and in his servant Moses. (Exodus 14:31)

Victoriously and trusting God, they took their first steps into the Red Sea and witnessed God's great power firsthand.

But just after the Red Sea miracle, they entered the desert. Water wasn't accessible for three days. When it was finally available to them, the flavor was bitter and they couldn't drink it. At this point, the Israelites grumbled and asked, "What are we supposed to drink? Did you bring us out here to die in the wilderness?"

So Moses turned to the Lord, who once again provided miraculously.

> He cried to the LORD, and the LORD showed him a log, and he
> threw it into the water, and the water became sweet. There the

LORD made for them a statute and a rule, and *there he tested them,* saying, "If you will diligently listen to the voice of the LORD your God, and do that which is right in his eyes, and give ear to his commandments and keep all his statutes, I will put none of the diseases on you that I put on the Egyptians, for I am the LORD, your healer." (15:25–26)

Desert Gifts

Maybe you are familiar with the Israelites' bitter water story. God clearly tested them to see if they trusted him. For me, a new truth unfolded in the next verse: "Then they came to Elim, where there were twelve springs of water and seventy palm trees, and they encamped there by the water" (verse 27).

Were they still in the desert? Yes. But God provided gifts in the desert. Out of nowhere, an oasis offered refreshment for their parched tongues and restoration for their tired bodies. These gifts infused them with the necessary strength to continue moving forward.

Do you find yourself in a place of waiting on God? Perhaps you are at the beginning of your trial and you've just discovered the bitter water. The bitterness has left you floundering to trust God through the wait. Maybe you are in the middle of your test, trying your hardest to find hydration. No matter your testing or trial, God has gifts for you right where you are. Smack-dab in the middle of your desert.

The gifts we unwrap in the desert are often the ones we appreciate the most.

When my kids have been outdoors playing hard on a sunny day, they are thankful for the water pitcher and cups I place out on the porch for them. On a cool, rainy day? Not as much. Have you ever noticed that water tastes the best when we need it the most?

Many times we feel like giving up because we are waiting on God and feel that he has forgotten us. And *we don't like it.* I find waiting on others difficult to do. If there is one thing I find hard to do for God, it is wait on him. I mean, isn't time valuable? Shouldn't he want us to move on with our next assignment? Why do we need to walk in desperate circles? Because we don't know the reason for the wait, we feel frustrated.

While I'm still learning how to wait patiently on God, I've combed his Word for hints on embracing this concept. When we find ourselves waiting in the desert, we can unwrap a few gifts to hydrate and nourish us.

The Gift of Strength

God has a purpose and plan for the desert. Waiting on God's move requires more character and strength than barging ahead on our own. The Bible encourages us to "wait for the LORD; be strong, and let your heart take courage; wait for the LORD!" (Psalm 27:14).

Our focus is often on the wait; God's focus is on the work. Through the process of the wait, we have the privilege of relying on him by choosing to read and believe his Word. Poised at opportunity's edge, we learn to listen to his direction by trusting that our Creator desires the best for us. Standing still, listening to his voice, and having our hearts open to his Word—these waiting activities provide and build strength. Each day we must take time to read and think through God's promises. We need to talk to him in prayer. We need to spend time listening to what the Holy Spirit would whisper to our hearts.

The Gift of Skills

If I gave my thirteen-year-old son a car for his birthday, what would happen? Most likely something horrible since he's not qualified to drive. He hasn't taken a single driving lesson. He doesn't know how the equipment functions. He barely understands how to unlock and start the car.

Untrained and unequipped, he lacks the necessary skills. If I gave him a car, he would have to wait until it is his time to learn to drive and he is prepared for the experience.

Immediate answers are wonderful, and sometimes God graciously provides in an instant. But many times we wait because God wants us to be equipped for the answer he's giving. As Paul tells us, "If we hope for what we do not see, we wait for it with patience" (Romans 8:25).

God knows how hard it would be to sit and stare at the answer while he continues to prepare us. So he gives us the time in the desert as an opportunity to be prepared. **The preparation God performs in us equips us for the privileges he provides.**

Many times when the test has passed and we've moved on to trust God, we glance backward and see the purpose of the difficulty. We recognize the skills we learned through the trial. Perhaps the skill is having patience. Maybe the skill is learning how to be gracious to others when waiting. Or what if the skill we learned is the ability to see God's love, even in the desert? No matter which skill was being developed, we gained maturity as a result of the test.

God alone knows when we are ready for the answer for which we've been waiting.

When we begin to view life from a faith-filled perspective, we can look back over the course of our journey and realize that God was there all along. We were not waiting without reason. Spiritual hindsight comes as we adjust our lenses to see as God sees. Although we can't see things to come, we can know that just as God had a purpose in the past, he can be trusted with the future.

The Gift of Support Through God's Word

Not only are we stuck in a desert, but that place can feel like the dreaded "waiting room." Fortunately, God's "waiting room" is not a room without action. The Bible tells us what to do while we wait: "I wait for the LORD, my soul waits, and in his word I hope" (Psalm 130:5).

To discover hope, we have to *be* in God's Word. To be in God's Word, we have to be intentional.

So whether you choose to participate in an online Bible study, or a community Bible study, or an individual Bible study, the type of study doesn't matter. Whether you follow a daily Bible reading plan, read through the Bible in a year, enjoy a chronological Bible, or read one verse a day in a devotional, the point is to purposefully engage in learning Scripture. God's Word is our support in the desert. When we find ourselves thirsty for encouragement, his promises hydrate our hearts. When we need spiritual refreshment, his Word provides the precise amount we need. What a gift!

The Gift of the Sense of His Presence

God longs to give us the answer we're searching for. Our hopes and dreams are not unnoticed by him. He sees our hearts and knows our wishes. He does not want us to give up. He loves us as his children and promises that just as we enjoy giving good gifts to our children, so also he wants to give good gifts to us. As the apostle James reminds us, "Every good gift and every perfect gift is from above, coming down from the Father of lights with whom there is no variation or shadow due to change" (1:17).

He really wants to give us something *much* bigger than the gift of our own hopes and dreams. **We want God to give us an answer; God wants to give us himself.**

He longs to draw us close in a relationship with him. When we are close to him, our desires will change. We won't want the same things we wanted before. Our desires are shaped and molded into new desires we hardly recognize. Knowing that he is with us and recognizing that his spirit never leaves us provides the patience we need while we wait for an answer. We might even forget all about that answer for which we are anxiously waiting, because we have found the answer in him.

A Ten-Year Desert

When Matt and I married, he worked the night shift. We agreed that a daytime schedule would be better for him and our family, but there were hurdles to changing the schedule. So we began to pray. And we prayed . . . and prayed . . . and prayed. It seemed like God had forgotten my husband, and the wait was long. I don't know how Matt functioned without sleep like he did or how he made it through the many church services, family functions, and social events.

After five years, Matt continued to work a full-time night shift while obtaining his second bachelor's degree *and* his master's degree. After ten years of praying, God gave him a new job with daytime hours. Ten years! But we were ecstatic.

I can look back over the journey and easily point out the strength God provided, the skills we learned, and the continual support of his Word, but it wasn't easy while we waited. The most precious gift in that desert of waiting was the knowledge that God was with us, no matter where the journey took us.

Sometimes from our perspective, the waiting and wandering in the desert continues pointlessly on and on. God never leaves us waiting on our own; he is always with us. How he longs to draw us close to him so that no matter our situation, no matter our desert, we can experience the gift of his presence. More than anything, he wants a close relationship with us. **What we often perceive as waiting is actually God's wooing.**

There are many circumstances in my life in which I'm waiting for God to help me see them as he sees them. I have issues I'm waiting on

God to change. But if there's one thing I've learned about waiting, it's this:

Waiting on God is always more than worth the wait.

～ ～ ～

Pillars of Truth to Lean On

When you want to give up and grow tired of waiting on God, lean on these truths.

- Have I not commanded you? Be strong and courageous. Do not be frightened, and do not be dismayed, for the LORD your God is with you wherever you go. (Joshua 1:9)
- Who is a rock, except our God?—the God who equipped me with strength and made my way blameless. (Psalm 18:31–32)
- Wait for the LORD; be strong, and let your heart take courage; wait for the LORD! (Psalm 27:14)
- For you, O LORD, do I wait; it is you, O Lord my God, who will answer. (Psalm 38:15)
- The LORD waits to be gracious to you, and therefore he exalts himself to show mercy to you. For the LORD is a God of justice; blessed are all those who wait for him. (Isaiah 30:18)

Stepping Stone #5

Waiting on God to change our circumstances or answer our prayers is difficult for anyone—especially because the desert-like conditions make us crave refreshment. Go to Stepping Stone #5 in your *One More Step* journal or make two columns on a sheet of paper. Label column one "instant" and column two "natural."

Write ten items under the "instant" column that reflect your favorite automatic solutions (for example: instant coffee, drive-through restaurants, instant mashed potatoes . . .). Then in the opposite column, list the slower, more natural comparison (fresh-brewed coffee, sit-down restaurants, Amish-style buttered mashed potatoes . . .).

At the bottom of each list, write this phrase:

"I am not waiting on God; I am being wooed to his side. May I enjoy every gift in this desert and draw closer to him. He is the answer, no matter the issue."

six

The Purpose Behind God's Plan

Never a trial that He is not there, never a burden
that He does not bear,
never a sorrow that He does not share,
moment by moment, I'm under His care.

—D. W. Whittle

After receiving Taylor's diagnosis of MPS, I finished asking God, "Where are we going?" It was evident that our desert would continue for years into the future. But a new persistent question haunted me in the night. This question caused my brain to spin and my heart to ache: *God, why?*

If you're reading this book, I'm sure you've asked God this question too. Perhaps many times.

Each of my children has gone through the preschool stage of asking the "why" question about everything. The kids aren't always satisfied with my answers. Sometimes I explain, "Because God made it that way." If you have ever experienced a child in the "why?" phase, then you know that her wish to understand the reason behind everything is part of the intellect God created within us. He designed our minds to be curious and creative. He uniquely designed various logical skills and thought processes.

But this desire to understand the world and everything in it can backfire on us. The desire for knowledge and understanding isn't a bad thing, but the actions we choose based on our knowing or not knowing is what gets us into trouble. We want to understand what God is doing in our lives—the purpose behind his plan—and when we don't understand it, we struggle with how to live through it.

Many times I would try to make plea bargains with God regarding Taylor's diagnosis. Surely it was a mistake and all this mess could just go away. He could fix it.

Is it something I've done? I would pray. *Because whatever it is, if you'll just show me how to make it right, then we can be finished with this thing. Is it something I need to do? If you'll just show me what I need to do, whatever it is, I'll do it.*

The feeling of wanting to give up often comes on us because it's so tough to comprehend what God is doing. We want so desperately to "get it all." We want to see just how it will all work out here on this earth. In this decade. Or this year. Or this week. Or this second.

We can't see the future. I know, that's a huge surprise to you.

Not only can I not see the future, but comprehending the present has grown difficult as well. Life looks insane at times. Evil lurks at every turn. The world appears totally corrupt and people can't be trusted. Society is messy and frayed. All this craziness causes me to look around and think, *Where is God in all this?*

Have you ever thought the same thing? In the midst of seeing pain, suffering, tragedy, cruelty, murder, rape, cancer, heart failure, adultery, or lying, have you ever just pondered, *God, where are you?*

The more I've reflected on this question, the more I've realized that the problem is not where God is. Because God is everywhere. The problem is that I'm asking the wrong question; I should be asking, *Why can't I see God in this?*

His fingerprints are all over his handiwork. Even when bad things happen to good people, he molds and reshapes until they can't even recognize the bad anymore. Many times we can't see immediate results in the reshaping, but he is creating a masterpiece, and masterpieces require time.

God's Incomprehensible Plan for Joseph

If there was ever a Bible character who should have given up, Joseph hits the target. His jealous brothers sold him into slavery and then deceived their father into believing a wild animal had killed him. Meanwhile, Joseph, shipped off to Egypt, was required to learn a new language, culture, and way of living. After encountering the drastic cultural change, Joseph experienced God's favor. "The LORD was with Joseph, and he became a successful man, and he was in the house of his Egyptian master" (Genesis 39:2).

Even Joseph's master, Potiphar, saw that God was with Joseph and that he was successful in everything he did. So Potiphar made Joseph boss over his entire household.

But then Potiphar's wife tried to seduce Joseph because she found him to be attractive. When he did not follow her bidding and instead put on his running shoes, she lied to her husband and claimed that he had raped her. Joseph found himself in prison, falsely accused. Once again Joseph saw God's hand on his life while enduring difficult circumstances: "But the LORD was with Joseph and showed him steadfast love and gave him favor in the sight of the keeper of the prison" (verse 21).

While in prison, Joseph interpreted a fellow prisoner's dream and requested that the man remember Joseph when he was restored to his former position. But when the cupbearer returned to his position, he forgot all about Joseph.

Joseph found himself waiting in prison for two more years. Two years! I think I would have been frustrated and would have wanted to give up. And maybe Joseph did; we don't know, since Scripture doesn't divulge Joseph's thoughts on his circumstances. However, after the two years, Joseph received a ticket out of jail.

At this time, Pharaoh had a dream and wanted an interpreter. In spite of calling on all the wise men in the country, Pharaoh could not get an answer about his dream's meaning. Finally, the cupbearer—Joseph's former fellow prisoner—came to the rescue. Remembering the service Joseph had provided him, he told Pharaoh about Joseph's interpreting skills.

Joseph was hurriedly pulled out of the prison pit and, after a quick shave, he was seated before the king to listen to his dream. Once he heard Pharaoh's dream, Joseph explained that God was the one who gave him the meanings of dreams. God delivered the dream's meaning to Joseph, who in turn delivered it to Pharaoh. Pharaoh's kingdom would experience seven years of bountiful harvest followed by seven years of famine. To provide for the years of famine, storehouses should be built and filled with grain. As a result of the dream's interpretation, Pharaoh placed Joseph second in charge of all of Egypt, with the specific duty to build, monitor, and fill those storehouses.

Wow. From the bottom of the pit to the top of the kingdom! Joseph experienced quite the contrasting titles. God graciously blessed Joseph, and years later when he had a son, he named the baby Manasseh, which means "God has made me forget all my hardship and all my father's house."

Even when bad things happen to good people, God is at work, orchestrating his good plans.

Joseph's heart and family were restored, but God wasn't finished yet. In the midst of the predicted famine years, Joseph's brothers came to

Egypt to buy grain. They were ushered before Joseph, whom they did not recognize. Yet he was fully aware of who they were.

Can you imagine how overwhelmed he felt in this moment? Based on the meaning of the name he had given his son, he had finally let go of his former life and his brothers' terrible actions against him. Now he faced them square in the eye. I doubt Joseph was excited to have an impromptu family reunion.

Although Joseph's story is filled with many more details, I want to share with you his final recorded words. Jacob, Joseph's father, had died, and Joseph's brothers feared that Joseph wanted to have their heads for selling him into slavery. But Joseph calmed their fears. He told them, "As for you, you meant evil against me, but God meant it for good, to bring it about that many people should be kept alive, as they are today" (Genesis 50:20).

God had done far more than Joseph ever thought possible. God had not only restored Joseph's heart, but he had also redeemed Joseph's relationship with his estranged family *and* prevented starvation in entire countries.

I've come to realize we aren't always going to understand God's plan because it's just so much bigger than we are.

I stopped asking the question, *God, where are you in all this?*
I started asking, *God, will you reveal yourself to me?*

Having learned from Joseph's story, now I simply pray, *Lord, help me see your work in this situation.*

I have to ponder what life would have been like for Joseph if he hadn't continued to trust God and seek him through the terrible circumstances he faced. I wonder if he felt like stomping his foot and telling God that life wasn't fair. Logically speaking, shouldn't life make sense? I mean, our brains are wired with a system of checks and balances. We are physically created with lefts and rights. Symmetry makes the world go 'round.

I think there is a reason that Joseph's statement about his brothers meaning evil but God redeeming it for good is not made until the end of the story.

Joseph didn't know that his years spent in slavery would position him to provide food for nations upon nations of people and prevent starvation of the masses. He didn't know that his brothers were going to bow down to him as a leader in Egypt. He didn't know that he would be reunited with his father and younger brother, whom he loved so much. He didn't understand God's plan until the plan came to fruition.

Even then, I have to wonder if Joseph sat back some days, staring at his children playing with their cousins, and thought, *How did this ever happen?* I wonder too if there were points in the story that we aren't privy to, maybe some times in which Joseph said to God, *"You want me to do what? Tell Pharaoh the meaning of his dream? But if I get it wrong, he'll cut off my head!"* While the Bible doesn't tell us that Joseph ever doubted God, because he was human, I'm sure he at least doubted himself.

What happens when we believe God is whispering to our hearts to do something that we can't wrap our heads around?

You see, God did not give us the ability to understand everything he does. Isaiah tells us that God's ways are higher than our ways (see 55:9). We cannot comprehend all that God does and why he does things the way he does them. Yet often we live in a frustrated state of asking God why and arguing with him about the means.

The Three Rs

Recently, I've had three words floating around in my mind regarding my obedience to his plan. These words call us back to the basics of obedience—the three Rs, if you will.

The first stage I've encountered in trying to follow what I believe

God would have me to do is not easy. In fact, many Christians don't make it past this step because it doesn't feel safe and we can't see what things look like up ahead.

Risking

To trust someone, anyone, even God, means you have to take a risk. In chapter 4, I described the factors of trusting God and believing that he is the God of the universe. The risking phase of following God's plan acknowledges that by faith, you have trusted him for salvation, and by faith, you believe that he is leading you to do something. **If we trust God for eternal salvation, then let's trust him for everyday solutions!**

I don't know what your "something" is. But I certainly know what mine has been and what it is currently. As I write this book, I feel like it's a big risk. *Did God really call me to write this book? What if no one reads it? What if I write words that people misunderstand? What if my heart is exposed and people question my intentions?*

Risk requires placing all your security and faith somewhere other than yourself. And this is where the risk is totally worth it. Because the risk you take is not a risk after all, since you place your security and faith in the God of the universe who loves the way he made you. He created you, and his relationship with you is the safest one you could ever have. His plans for you exceed your imagination, and he is actively working in your life. While you may not understand his plan, like Joseph, you can have faith that he is with you and his plan is the best one for you. God's rate of return on investments is never a risk because he guarantees every life experience will be used for good. The risk you feel like you are taking actually has zero chance of failure when you allow God to work freely in and through it. As Paul says, "No eye has seen, nor ear heard, nor the heart of man imagined, what God has prepared for those who love him" (1 Corinthians 2:9).

Releasing

Releasing is the letting-go phase. This is when we decide that not only are we going to take the risk and make the move we feel impressed to make, but we are going to let go of whatever we grip in place of God's hand. Maybe we've had enough of what the world is offering, and we decide to exchange it for what God offers. Or we're worn out from carrying our broken dreams, and we decide to place everything in God's hands rather than continuing to bear the burden alone.

An example of this phase is giving God an offering from the last dollar in the bank when we don't know where the next one is coming from. Or giving our packed lunch to a homeless person when it's all we have for the day. Maybe it's moving to another city, far from home, as Joseph was forced to do. Perhaps the release is giving God a relationship gone sour, a broken heart, or an incurable disease. No matter the item or issue, the release is giving it to God. It's a stance with open palms before the Savior, indicating that my hands no longer grasp for what cannot satisfy.

Releasing is giving up whatever I'm clutching, including the inability to understand his plan. It's telling God that I'm finished thinking I know more than he does. **Releasing my grasp of all things temporal allows the grip of God to become most real to me.**

Nothing we endure on this earth will last forever. When we let go of temporary problems, we begin to realize the permanent value of God's eternal answers. And when we've released whatever it is that we're holding, we are blessed to enter the third phase of following his plan and process.

Rejoicing

You see, if we never take the risk, if we never consider that he who saved us wants to redeem us, if we never release our lives to him and accept his plan, then we miss the rejoicing phase. We bypass the opportunity to experience joy flooding our souls as we join God in his plan, whatever it may be. We can enjoy overflowing happiness when we believe that God is who he says he is and that he is going to keep his Word because he has never failed to do so. As Isaiah reminds us, "Remember the former things of old; for I am God, and there is no other; I am God, and there is none like me, declaring the end from the beginning and from ancient times things not yet done, saying, 'My counsel shall stand, and I will accomplish all my purpose'" (46:9–10).

The God who is taking us to heaven wants to use us on this earth.

Why does God want to use us?

It is not logical.

It is love.

Reaping the Rewards of His Plan

The real estate agent unlocked another home for Matt, Taylor, and me to enter. After walking through each room, I could hardly believe it: God was answering our prayers for a house! As we pulled out of the driveway, four-year-old Taylor began to sing as she did so often. Her beautiful voice sweetly sounded every word to "Jesus Loves Me." It was breathtaking.

We moved into that very house, and a year and a half later, Taylor lost her ability to talk. As the days passed, her sweet voice stopped connecting with her brain, and before I knew it, her precious ability to sing had disappeared as well.

I felt it was risky business to trust God with Taylor's speech loss. Wouldn't it be better if she could communicate easily? Wouldn't life be better with her voice intact?

I can't say that I took the risk to give God Taylor's speech loss as soon as it happened. I would try to give it to God, and then I'd grab the fear and worry back and squeeze it tightly to my chest. As much as I ached to hear Taylor call me Mommy just one more time, I finally decided to believe that God's plan included Taylor's loss of language. I have risked that in spite of my inability to understand God's plan, I believe his Word. I've chosen to trust that his plan for Taylor is far beyond what my mind can fathom and he knows what is best for her. I've made the choice to believe that his plan is bigger than Taylor's inability to speak or sing and that we simply cannot comprehend his incredible love for her. I've pried my fingers open and released her voice loss to him. I release my fears of the future to him daily. As a result, I rest and rejoice in his promises, such as Peter's description in 1 Peter 5:10: "After you have suffered a little while, the God of all grace, who has called you to his eternal glory in Christ, will himself restore, confirm, strengthen, and establish you."

If I focus, if I try my hardest to remember what that day was like when she sang, I can still hear her precious little voice singing, "Little ones to him belong, they are weak but he is strong." I'm reminded that one day in heaven, I'll understand his plan and hear her voice again. Until then, I have the strength to take one more step.

～ ～ ～

Pillars of Truth to Lean On

When I struggle to understand why God allows certain things to happen, I hold on to these promises as a reminder that my ability to understand is limited, but God's plan is unlimited.

- Know therefore that the LORD your God is God, the faithful God who keeps covenant and steadfast love with those who love him and keep his commandments, to a thousand generations. (Deuteronomy 7:9)
- Great is our Lord, and abundant in power; his understanding is beyond measure. (Psalm 147:5)
- Have you not known? Have you not heard? The LORD is the everlasting God, the Creator of the ends of the earth. He does not faint or grow weary; his understanding is unsearchable. (Isaiah 40:28)
- My thoughts are not your thoughts, neither are your ways my ways, declares the LORD. For as the heavens are higher than the earth, so are my ways higher than your ways and my thoughts than your thoughts. (Isaiah 55:8-9)
- It is God who works in you, both to will and to work for his good pleasure. (Philippians 2:13)

Stepping Stone #6

Understanding God's complete and total design for our lives is not humanly possible. Our finite minds can't grasp every detail of the Creator's plan. Choose one of the verses from the list above to memorize and to reinforce your belief that we can rest and rejoice in his promises. Write it down five times in the *One More Step* journal on Stepping Stone #6. Read this verse aloud for thirty days and retain it as a stepping stone to remembering that God's plan is bigger and better than yours.

seven

The Necessary Grace

'Twas grace that taught my heart to fear, and
grace my fears relieved.

—John Newton

To watch someone you love slowly lose her ability to communicate is heartrending. At age five, Taylor pronounced her last full sentence when her younger brother was born. Her little eyes stared at the sight of this new wiggly bundle, and her understanding of the birth all meshed together with her words: *This is Michael. I'm a big sister.* The following summer, Taylor said her last intelligible words: *ice cream.*

I asked God why again. I felt that I was being punished for sin in my own life, and I begged God to show me what it was.

I bartered with God: *Lord, if you'll just show me what I need to do to make things right, I'll do it. Whatever it is. You tell me what I need to change, and I'll change it. Anything to keep my baby girl from going through this slow daily torture. Please don't make her go through this. Please don't make us go through this.*

I begged God to remove Taylor's trouble. And because I am her mama, her disease was my heartache also. There was no cure and no medical treatment in sight. If you've watched someone close to you suffer, then you understand how much I wanted to take Taylor's suffering away.

In reply to my pleadings, I felt God's whisper to my heart: *My grace is sufficient for you. You can't imagine the work I'm going to do through this journey, but my plan and my power are far greater than you know. The end result is going to be beyond your imagination, and everything is going to be perfect.*

I started to understand that his grace overpowers burdens. That he could carry us through anything we would endure.

Gradually I began to tell God how much I needed him, that there was no way we could go through this without him. If he wasn't going to change the circumstance, I needed his strength to get through it. I started to sense his presence giving me strength when I had none. I began to notice pictures of grace from him, like teachers who cared for Taylor, bus drivers who faithfully ensured her safety, and therapists who wanted to help Taylor be the best she could be. Slowly, step by step, I accepted that his plan for our lives included Taylor's MPS. With his grace, he covered me. But without his grace—the hints of understanding that he was with us—I had no idea how we could pick up our weary feet and take one more step.

As Ann Voskamp wrote in *One Thousand Gifts,* "Sometimes you don't know when you're taking the first step through a door until you're already inside."[1] I stood at the door of grace when MPS entered Taylor's life. I can't remember the exact moment I stepped through. All I know is that once I made it across the threshold, I've wanted more understanding of his grace, and he has always provided.

Grace—One Size Fits All

A small box, delicately wrapped and left on the bed by my college roommate, caught my gaze as soon as I walked in the room. I could only dream of what was inside. My name was on the box; did this mean I could open it? Maybe it didn't. What if it was chocolate? I could have really gone for some dark chocolate right then. It sat for a few minutes until I could no longer cope with curiosity. Every nerve in my body chanted, *O-pen it. O-pen it.*

I removed the silk ribbon and tugged at the tape. Anticipation was building and I dreamed of a bracelet or earrings or something else pretty. I ripped open the box to find something wrapped in pink tissue paper. This had to be a good sign, right?

I found a pair of pantyhose. Nice.

Not that I didn't need the pantyhose—we're talking the 1980s, when decorative legwear and leg warmers were all the rage. But these were the itchy, funky kind. No dainty decorative flowers or black lace design. No bright neon colors or opaque plaid. Just itchy, orangish-nude pantyhose that looked like sunless tanning lotion gone bad. And to beat that, I couldn't find a size on the package. Finally, I saw a tag sticking out of the top of the hose that read "One Size Fits All."

Seriously? So six-foot Susie from two doors down could wear the same size as my five-foot-five frame? Funny thing is that I actually wound up using those pantyhose one day when mine snagged and I had no backup.

I don't know anyone who doesn't like to receive gifts—I mean the really good, I-wish-I-had-one kind of gifts. But giving great gifts often requires forethought, don't you think? You have to think it through. Plan. Make choices. Be purposeful. Shop. Wrap. Give.

And the very best kinds of gifts? They are not tangible. The best gifts are typically wrapped inside of hearts rather than paper. Love is a beautiful gift. Peace? Ah, peace is such a gift. Joy is a gift that can't necessarily be held in your hand. Grace is truly one of those gifts. **Grace takes many shapes, yet one size fits all.**

I don't mean the pantyhose kind of "one size fits all." There are no extra folds creased over at the top. The toes don't have extra fabric, twisted into knots to use up the excess. The center of the hose between the legs doesn't cause the most uncomfortable gap in fit known to womankind. You know what I'm talking about? No, grace is truly something each of us needs, especially when we feel like giving up.

We've discovered the grace of God lavished on Old Testament figures, some of whom we've mentioned in previous chapters. But when did the entire world receive the gift of God's grace? The grace of God was visibly revealed when Jesus arrived on earth in human form: "For God so loved the world, that he gave his only Son" (John 3:16).

This was the beginning of our grace gift: *God gave.* He gave because he loved. And because he loved, he gave. God's beautiful grace is a cycle, a circle of loving and giving.

As sure as John 3:16 tells us God gave, the Bible is equally clear that we are saved by God's grace. That is what grace does: grace saves. As Paul says in Ephesians 2:8, "For by grace you have been saved through faith. And this is not your own doing; it is the gift of God."

The world's greatest gift exchange is humanity's sin for God's grace.

God wants to give us so much more than the initial grace we accepted when we trusted Christ as our Savior. Paul provided us with insight as to how this fact played out in his own life. While we don't know the exact details of Paul's issue, he described his problem as "a thorn [that] was given me in the flesh" (2 Corinthians 12:7). Interestingly enough, every Bible translation I read used the same word description of "a thorn in the flesh." He had some type of physical ailment that nearly drove him crazy. Many believe that he suffered from a sight problem. Whatever it was, Paul wanted it removed!

In his second letter to the church at Corinth, Paul explained to the Corinthians that he had asked God three times to remove the issue from him. But God's answer to him was not a whisking-away, problem-vanishing solution. No magic eraser, Spot Shot spot remover, or delete button.

Though God has the power to provide immediate healing, he also possesses wisdom for the timing of the healing. His answer to Paul reveals one of the miraculous secrets of giving our burdens to the Lord: "My grace is sufficient for you, for my power is made perfect in weakness" (verse 9).

God was teaching Paul the very lesson he wants us to learn. **The situations we wish God would remove from our lives are often the lessons God uses to teach us to rely on him.**

The problems, circumstances, and frustrations we can't handle are what give God the most glory in our lives when we give them to him. Without the circumstance or burden, as we see it, we wouldn't be drawn into a closer relationship with God. His grace ushers in strength for when we feel like giving up. When we recognize our inability to make it through the trials on our own, then we begin to see how much we need his preserving grace. When others see how God is carrying us through our trials, then he is glorified.

Max Lucado reminds us that "sustaining grace promises not the absence of struggle but the presence of God."[2] God's grace allows us to look beyond the current anguish to gain the perspective of his presence. We then realize that he is always with us, and with God, we can face any situation life brings.

Grace came to Paul in the form of a "thorn in the flesh," a physical ailment that he begged God to remove. God told Paul that his grace was bigger than Paul's problem, big enough to carry the apostle through the pain and suffering. Though Paul couldn't see it, the end result would be more than a resolved problem; it would be consecrated perfection.

The second half of 2 Corinthians 12:9, which highlights Paul's realization, began to reflect itself in my heart: "Therefore I will boast all the more gladly of my weaknesses, so that the power of Christ may rest upon me." **I realized God wants to do more than change my situation; he wants to change my heart.** Oddly enough, I felt the most strength and the most peace when I started sharing with others what Christ was doing in Taylor's life and in my heart. And in between the thorn and grace, joy showed up.

One Way Joy Showed Up

In 2008, a few weeks before Thanksgiving, the worship pastor at my church made an announcement to the choir and orchestra during rehearsal. He requested volunteers to share their testimonies for use in the upcoming Christmas musical. His idea was simply to share stories of how God was working in the lives of choir and orchestra members, which would uplift the spirits of those attending the musical. He encouraged us to take a few moments and send him an e-mail of what God was doing in our hearts.

I knew he was speaking to me. So the next morning, as soon as I had a few minutes, I typed out an e-mail about Taylor's diagnosis and how our family had been processing the journey of her terminal illness. I emphasized that while I didn't have everything figured out, I knew that God was using Taylor to draw me closer to him. Matt and I had no doubt that God created Taylor with the same purpose as everyone else in the world—to glorify himself.

The phone rang later that day, and when I answered, I heard the voice of the worship pastor's assistant. She told me that when the pastor received my e-mail, his heart was touched. The assistant wanted to know if she could record a video interview and add photos to tell a five-minute version of our story about God's glory. So we recorded the testimony and they showed the video in all four Christmas musical services. By the end of the services, forty-eight people signed cards to say that they accepted Christ as their Savior!

God's immense grace brings joy in the midst of suffering.

A certain doctor was at church that week for the first time in years. His neighbor had invited his family to the musical. As an atheist, the man had no interest in coming to the service, but for the sake of his family, he chose to attend with them. His name was on one of those cards. When a friend asked him why he finally chose to accept God in his life, he replied, "That woman's faith in the video story was real."

It's so crazy to think that God could bring such joy between the thorn and grace.

Extending Grace

Extending grace to ourselves when we make mistakes is critical to curbing the emotions that flood our souls when we are ready to throw in the towel. I find that often the hardest person to give grace to is me. I want to fix the problem, not live with it. While it's wonderful to overcome issues, circumstances that are out of our jurisdiction must be covered in grace. Giving grace might look like promising to do better next time instead of internally degrading ourselves. Or choosing to focus on a positive response rather than the out-of-control circumstance. Maybe grace looks like going to bed early when we are getting too tired or forgiving ourselves when we make a mistake.

For grace to make her entrance, she has to be willingly offered and mercifully issued. Then when we recognize our own shortcomings and failures, we can realize the grace gift we've so wonderfully been given and accept it for ourselves. **Grace is not only a gift from God; grace is a gift to extend to others.**

Speaking about the grace of God is glorious. Extending God's gracious gift of salvation is beautiful. But as a Christian, I don't want the grace I offer to stop there. Oh, it's easy to offer grace to those I see who need Christ's love. But I've found that I often draw the line at offering grace to one who has personally offended me, especially someone I think should know better as a Christian. I fail to extend grace because my feelings have been hurt.

Failure to extend grace results in the growth of bitterness. When fostered, its roots can grow as strong as the roots of hope. Resentment can even overtake those roots of hope we worked so hard to foster at the beginning. When we use our energy to latch on to bitterness, our determination to withhold grace winds up zapping our strength.

Withholding grace seems justifiable when I've done nothing wrong. But by doing so, I completely miss the point of grace. Grace holds healing power.

Giving grace hasn't always been a priority for me. In fact, for most of my life as a Christian, extending grace to others was an afterthought, if that. I'm embarrassed to admit this, but it's the truth. Many of the rules and regulations kept me so preoccupied with my little checklist of whether or not I was doing right that I completely missed opportunities to reflect God's light. Have you ever experienced a season when the focus on rules turned into judgment? I had created a standard that couldn't be kept. By anyone. Ever.

Eventually I came to understand that God's grace is meant to be shared. Grace is a transferable, renewing resource. God gives it to us and then we give it to others, and before you know it, a circle of love has formed—all by grace. You see, when we accept the grace of God over our own lives, for salvation, for mistakes, we agree that God's way is the best way. And that his grace is for all—not just for us to hoard. As Paul reminds us, "It is all for your sake, so that as grace extends to more and more people it may increase thanksgiving, to the glory of God" (2 Corinthians 4:15).

The questions then become: With whom am I to share grace? Who needs grace from me today? Right now. A coworker who doesn't perform his job well? A parent who made mistakes in parenting? A spouse who made a wrong turn? A child who needs my love? A relative who is caught in the trap of selfishness?

When nothing else can reach hurting hearts, grace reaches.

Grace has properties unlike any physical, tangible object because grace is from God. Grace is a liquid that can take on the shape of its container. Grace is a solid that is locked into place. Grace has the property of gas; it flows freely.

Maybe grace looks like giving a coworker a hand, even when she's never helped you. Could it possibly appear as offering kindness to that relative who has a terrible disease known as diarrhea of the mouth? Perhaps grace could look like giving that person a gift when he's done nothing but condemn your ideas. Could it appear by being all right with someone else's differences, by agreeing to disagree? Maybe, just maybe, grace looks like Jesus because it is Jesus. "For if many died through one man's [Adam's] trespass, much more have the grace of God and the free gift by the grace of that one man Jesus Christ abounded for many" (Romans 5:15).

With God's grace in us, we possess the gift that truly continues to give. When we allow God's grace to permeate us, we can extend grace to both ourselves and others.

One of the greatest ways to extend grace is to pray for one another. Paul declared that the beautiful prayer gift of grace is beyond words. "[They will] pray for you, because of the surpassing grace of God upon you. Thanks be to God for his inexpressible gift!" (2 Corinthians 9:14–15).

Recently a situation occurred that angered me greatly. I was mad because it was unjust, unfair, and I didn't deserve the words this person had hurled my way. But I didn't think the lady would listen to me, because she saw the matter only from her perspective. So with words seeming to be completely inadequate and no idea of what else I could do, I began to pray. Before the afternoon passed, the woman called me and apologized.

Now, you'll probably think I have little faith, but I was shocked that God answered my prayer. The woman was not known for her humility, and I had told God I was prepared to forgive her and overlook the entire incident. I requested his grace to do so. And just when I did, his grace showed up in a totally different way—through her request to be forgiven.

It was as if God were saying to me, *It's okay, girl. I've got this one. You don't have to wear this uncomfortable pair of pantyhose pulled up to your armpits. We're going to let this go.*

When I struggled to move forward, grace allowed for one more step. Isn't grace such a gift?

Grace from God takes many shapes, yet one size fits all. Grace says, *You don't have to be qualified or adequately equipped.* Grace says, *Come to me as you are. I've got this.* God anticipates slathering grace all over your life; he simply desires a willing heart.

Ah, yes. Grace fits so much better than a cheap pair of pantyhose.

～ ～ ～

Pillars of Truth to Lean On

This list of verses is one I enjoy when I need to remember God's gift of grace.

- Give ear, O LORD, to my prayer; listen to my plea for grace. (Psalm 86:6)
- From his fullness we have all received, grace upon grace. For the law was given through Moses; grace and truth came through Jesus Christ. (John 1:16–17)
- I do not account my life of any value nor as precious to myself, if only I may finish my course and the ministry that I received from the Lord Jesus, to testify to the gospel of the grace of God. (Acts 20:24)
- Through him we have also obtained access by faith into this grace in which we stand, and we rejoice in hope of the glory of God. (Romans 5:2)

Stepping Stone #7

Accepting God's grace and receiving it for ourselves infuses strength within us when we feel like giving up. Write down three areas of life in which you know you are extra hard on yourself and you need to give yourself grace. Pray over this list and then write down your prayer to God over these three issues. Next write down the name(s) of someone you know who needs your grace. Add it to the written prayer for Stepping Stone #7 in your *One More Step* journal. Great job on taking another step to finding strength for the journey of life!

eight

Overcoming the Overwhelming

He is my strength from day to day, without
Him I would fall.

—Will L. Thompson

Some days out of habit, I would pick up the phone to call her, only to
realize a second later that I couldn't. She was gone.

Once Mom graduated to heaven, one of my favorite months of the
year became one of the most difficult: May. Mom's birthday was May 10.
Since Mother's Day is always close to that date, going to church on Mother's
Day became bittersweet. My heart's desire was to celebrate the children
God had given me and the joys of being a mother. But at the same
time, I ached to see my mama and enjoy one of our old days of spreading
fabric out on the living room floor to pin and cut sewing patterns.

To make matters worse, six-year-old Taylor gradually was losing cognitive
discernment. She didn't sleep well, and when she woke up in the
night, she'd play quietly in her room. Some nights, I placed her back in
bed so many times that I couldn't hold my eyes open long enough to walk
to her room one more time. I'd sleep on the floor in the hallway to ensure
that she didn't injure herself or leave her room. We had made everything
as childproof as we could. We moved the light switch to the outer hallway
so she wouldn't play with it. To keep her from harming herself by

swinging on hangers and climbing on closet shelves, we placed locks on the closet doors.

Then she developed a habit of placing her hands in her diaper. During the day, we kept a close eye on her diapering needs, but at night, it became more difficult.

One Sunday morning, I awoke early to prepare for church. Before I hopped in the shower, I peeked in on Taylor. In spite of my early rising, Taylor had apparently been awake for a while. She had taken on an art project of the worst kind. Because I had been unable to care for her diapering needs instantly, she had plastered the room with poop. Everything her hands had touched since placing them in her diaper was affected. The curtains, the walls, the bedding, the carpet, the doorknob, her toys. Everything.

I could hardly pull myself together enough emotionally to take her to the bathtub and wash her clean. Then I opened her bedroom window, closed the door, and took her to my bed to watch TV so I could take a speed shower. All the while, I sobbed and asked God why.

Why did we have to go through this? Why did she have to lose her mind? Why did I have to spend the afternoon after church scrubbing down the entire room?

And why did all this have to happen on Mother's Day?

I couldn't do it. I didn't want to be a mom. I didn't want to be Taylor's mom.

I was overwhelmed on every level and struggled to understand. *Why does life have to be so difficult?*

Overwhelming Situations

As if the hurts, heartache, and problems are not enough, the daily routine can easily shift into a daily grind. Sometimes we struggle to find the joy of everyday living in the midst of tough circumstances because life is happening quickly and issues pile up. On top of just trying to make it through a day, interruptions pop up like uninvited guests. Circumstances don't just threaten to overwhelm; they succeed in doing so.

Feeling overwhelmed so often prevents us from taking the next step; it makes us want to give up. While reflecting on the causes, I discovered two scenarios in which we often feel overwhelmed.

The first is when issues stack up against you and you feel you can no longer manage. In the midst of caring for a sick family member, financial crisis hits. Without money to pay medical bills, the family member is unable to receive his much-needed medical care. Instead of getting well, he gets worse. In the midst of this, a different family member is in a car accident and has to be hospitalized for two weeks. While he is hospitalized, his family struggles to pay their bills and asks you for help. You want to help but don't know how you can.

When the waves continue to beat us up without a break, then we flat out feel overwhelmed.

The second reason we can feel overwhelmed is not a gradual issue. In fact, things seem to be going well until one day, a life tsunami hits. Completely and totally unexpected. We had no time to prepare.

It could be that your spouse walked in and told you there is another. Perhaps you are thirty-five years old, and you just discovered you were adopted. Instead of an ebb and flow to life, you feel caught up in an unforgiving riptide.

How can we prevent the magnitude of situations and circumstances from overwhelming us to the point of giving up? When the *This is just too hard* thought first enters our brains, how can we cope with the realization that the problem is bigger than we are? At this point, how can we possibly discover strength?

Tempting Solutions to Overwhelming Situations

When overwhelming situations arise, we need to remember that the Enemy is eagerly waiting for the right moment to pounce on us in our weaknesses. As 1 Peter 5:8 reminds us, "Be sober-minded; be watchful. Your adversary the devil prowls around like a roaring lion, seeking someone to devour."

Before we can address how to find strength in overwhelming situations, we must first identify how Satan pounces on us, especially when we are overwhelmed. See if you can relate to any of the temptations below.

The Temptation to Listen to the Enemy's Lies

Listening to Satan's lies was the first mistake Eve made in the garden. She paused long enough to hear his words, he took advantage of her listening ears, and the rest is obviously history. When Satan throws his seductive lies your way, fight back with the truth of God's Word! For example, when Satan whispers to your mind, *You can't do this,* respond with the power God has given us and say, "I am more than a conqueror because of Christ." Here are some other examples:

Satan's Lies	God's Truth
You're weak and need to stop.	The LORD is my strength and my shield (Psalm 28:7).
This situation is impossible.	With God all things are possible (Matthew 19:26).
It's just too much; you'll never make it.	We are more than conquerors through him (Romans 8:37).
You can't do this.	I can do all things through him who strengthens me (Philippians 4:13).
You are going to fail.	God gave us a spirit not of fear (2 Timothy 1:7).

The Temptation to Isolate Ourselves from God and Fellow Christians

Satan wants us to feel alone in our distress. When we listen to him, we tell ourselves, "It's only this one church service. I can watch it online." Before we know it, we've missed four weeks of church and haven't read our Bible in months.

Certainly, there's nothing wrong with taking time alone and being still. In fact, I'm a huge proponent of using quiet time to refuel. But we can't leave God out of the quiet time! Being overwhelmed can prompt us to block out everything and everyone, including God. We're tempted to build walls around our hearts for "protection," but the walls also prevent the benefits of fellowship, like love, joy, and strength.

The Temptation to Fall into Poor Physical Health Habits

The easiest thing to do when we feel overwhelmed is overindulge. The worst thing to do when we feel overwhelmed is overindulge.

Maybe your temptation is to escape with alcohol, drugs, or even an overdose of chocolate. Or perhaps you know you have a tendency to drink double the caffeine and regret it later when a headache latches on. To combat this behavior, ask someone close to be your accountability partner or keep a log of how much coffee or soda you are drinking. If you are tempted to take refuge in an unhealthy physical routine, run the opposite direction. Abusing or neglecting your body in any manner drains your stamina.

If your temptation is to lie around and do nothing, then you miss the natural hormonal processes that strengthen your resolve to persevere. Take a brisk walk around the neighborhood or engage in a physical activity you normally enjoy.

The Temptation to Make Poor Mental Health Choices

Choosing your mental intake is especially important when you feel over-whelmed. If you enjoy relaxing in front of the TV for a few minutes and use it as a tool to unwind, that's understandable. Or maybe you love to wind down by playing games on your tablet or electronic device, but you later regret that you wasted too much time playing. No matter the device, if you find yourself feeling even more overwhelmed after engaging, Satan has successfully detoured you from fighting the battle. We've all heard "Garbage in; garbage out." On the flip side, saturating our minds with Scripture or listening to worship music positively affects our mental health.

The Temptation to Escape to Social Media

Social media is an easy escape for many of us. We can read, comment, and share almost anything we desire instantly. Social media often serves as our connection to the world, which can convert into an escape from our internal problems. One of the issues with combining social media ab-sorption and an upset heart is that we can find ourselves in a trap of com-parison. *Why do the Joneses have it so easy? I don't think anyone in their family ever gets sick. Those Browns never have a care in the world.*

Another issue is that we can use it as a complaint station to air our feelings and discover later that we didn't truly mean what we posted. Closely guarding both what we read and post on social media can prevent feelings of being overcome with stress.

The Temptation to Escape to Retail Therapy

Perhaps your favorite method of dealing with stress is to head to the mall and shop till you drop. Maybe you don't head to the mall but instead waste three hours on shopping websites or making wish lists for future transactions. If this is your temptation, set up an accountability partner so you simply can't go there.

Satan is watching for your weak moment—the perfect timing to hit you with temptations of all sorts, anything that will prevent you from finding the strength you need to overcome the overwhelming. Be aware of his temptations. As James reminds us, "Resist the devil, and he will flee from you" (4:7).

If you find yourself addicted to unhealthy choices, run to Jesus and seek professional advice. God provides the strength you need when the waves of life engulf you, and he uses people to help him. Call a trusted loved one or friend. Contact your pastor or make an appointment with a Christian counselor. Whatever the overpowering temptation, just take one more step: recognize the problem and search for someone who can help you.

True Strength for Overwhelming Situations

A well-known Bible character, David certainly led a fascinating life, complete with both successes and failures. When David was anointed king of Israel, everyone thought Samuel, the priest God sent to perform the dedication, had the wrong guy. Although he was anointed at a young age, David did not actually become king until years later. He spent the years in between hiding and running from his enemies, especially King Saul. As a result of this season in David's life, we are privileged to have Psalm 18.

Many psalm subtitles outline the psalm's author or the tune to which it was sung. As I was poring over Psalms, I discovered the description that accompanies Psalm 18 provides an incredible backdrop to assist us in comprehending how overwhelming David's situation was just before he wrote it. The description reads:

To the choirmaster. A Psalm of David, the servant of the LORD, who addressed the words of this song to the LORD on the day

when the LORD rescued him from the hand of all his enemies,
and from the hand of Saul.

The fights and flights were too many to count between David's anointing and the moment he took reign over Israel. Scholars differ in their projections for this time period, but regardless of the number of years, David lived in overwhelming, life-threatening circumstances. If Psalm 18 were written today, it might be known as "David's Survival Guide for the Overwhelmed." Let's take a look at his tips for overcoming the overwhelming.

David's Survival Guide for the Overwhelmed

Tip #1: Recognize that God is the source of your strength.
After reading the description of Psalm 18, I love that David's first words in the psalm were, "I love you, O LORD, my strength."

David had long known where true strength for the battle lay. His first words of this beautiful psalm gave God the full praise and recognition for being the source of his strength. His declaration of love preceded any other words, and his example of praise is one we can emulate.

Tip #2: Realize that prayer is your lifeline.
David prayed to God in praise, he prayed in distress, and he prayed when he needed help. No matter his state of being, his first action was to call on the Lord.

I call upon the LORD, who is worthy to be praised. . . . In my
distress I called upon the LORD; to my God I cried for help. From
his temple he heard my voice, and my cry to him reached his ears.
(verses 3, 6)

If we are in a habit of praying regularly, then when that overwhelmed feeling threatens us, our prayer reflex will kick in automatically. This is why keeping an open lifeline to God is so important. We need it continually, and our heavenly Father loves to hear from us. As it says in Psalm 66:20, "Blessed be God, because he has not rejected my prayer or removed his steadfast love from me!" **Prayer should be our first response, not our last resort.**

What does your prayer life look like right now? Would your prayer in this moment be a first response or a last resort?

Tip #3: Remember the victories God gave in the past.
David reminisced over the journey and all God had enabled him to do. The victories from the past encouraged his steps toward the future. "For by you I can run against a troop, and by my God I can leap over a wall. . . . The God who equipped me with strength and made my way blameless" (Psalm 18:29, 32).

What has God brought you through so far? How does this encourage your heart to know that he will give you the strength to take one more step?

Tip #4: Refuse to focus on personal limitations and believe God will do his redemptive work in you.
David was just a shepherd boy, but God saw him as so much more. David's heart trusted the Lord to do through him what he could not do alone. "He made my feet like the feet of a deer and set me secure on the heights. He trains my hands for war, so that my arms can bend a bow of bronze" (verses 33–34).

David, the shepherd boy, became a mountain climber. The knowledge of God as his strength infused David's body, and physical strength became his ally.

When I pondered these two verses, the thought came to me that maybe David had acrophobia, also known as "a fear of heights." Regardless, God steadied his footsteps, even at high altitudes.

What personal fears are holding you back from believing God will empower you for his work? What past failures need to be released into his forgiving hands?

Tip #5: Recall the details of God's moment-by-moment provisions.

David's famous fight against Goliath was his first step from shepherd to warrior. Whether his battle gear consisted of five smooth stones or full armor, he knew God was the one who preserved him. "You have given me the shield of your salvation, and your right hand supported me, and your gentleness made me great" (verse 35).

Not only was David thankful for overall strength, but he tallied up the details of how the victory was made possible. He noted the protection, support, and gentleness of God throughout this entire overwhelming period.

How has God provided protection for you in your overwhelming circumstances? Is there a blessing from him that you can see even in the midst of the pain?

Tip #6: Renew your perspective of the situation.

As mentioned in Tip #4, David felt the stability of God in his footsteps. In addition to the steadiness, he explained that his vision of the mountainside changed from narrow and dangerous to wide and safe: "You gave a wide place for my steps under me, and my feet did not slip. I pursued my enemies and overtook them, and did not turn back till they were consumed. . . . For you equipped me with strength for the battle" (verses 36–37, 39).

God widened David's tunnel vision and gave him the ability to see that this path wasn't as narrow as he thought. David's fear of falling dissipated when he realized that the spaces for his steps were more than ample. His strength didn't come from himself; he had access to the inexhaustible source of strength from God.

Can you see that the path God has for you is more than wide enough for your next step? Is your vision limited by failing to recognize his never-ending supply of strength?

My perspective of being an overwhelmed mama has changed drastically since that Mother's Day afternoon I spent cleaning up poop. I've learned that God is my total source of strength and that by continually talking to my heavenly Father about everything, I will naturally take my burdens to him as well. When I think about the victories God has given me by providing patience and understanding, I'm stunned by his provision. I stopped focusing on my lack of abilities to care for a child with special needs and began comprehending that God chose me to be Taylor's mother. I am the mom he trusts with her unique and precious life.

Like David, it has been and continues to be a journey for me. That's why it's called a survival guide. We're likely going to need the reminders again and again, right?

From Beaten Down to Building Up

After several more poopy incidents, God gave me an idea. Taylor could unzip her footie pajamas from the front. And she could undress herself faster than the world record. But what if I modified the pajamas?

I took two of her old pairs, cut off the foot portion of each pajama leg, and sewed them back on backward. She could take off her socks and would often chew on them, so the feet needed to be on the pajamas. But by switching them around, the zipper portion of the pajamas was in the back instead of the front. Taylor could no longer undress herself and put her hand in her diaper. And the "Hallelujah Chorus" rang out!

Many years later, I sat at a women's Bible study table in one of my first leadership roles as a discussion facilitator. One particular morning, a young mom slid into her seat at our table. She was about a half-hour late for the study and visibly upset. When we had a moment to connect, she told our small group about the dilemma of her morning. Her almost two-year-old son had learned how to undress. That morning he not only had undressed but also had decided to become the Picasso of Poo and paint everything within reach. While the lady seemed embarrassed over the situation, she was also desperate. We gave her time to explain the completely understandable frustration, and as she talked, I was taken back to that awful Mother's Day when I stood in her shoes. When she finished her explanation, I gave her a kind smile and let her know that, unfortunately, I had experience in this particular parenting department.

I asked her if she had any footie pajamas for him, which she did. I outlined the official pajama modification process. When she left the Bible study, she was fully prepared to execute the plan to annihilate poopy baby art.

Just a couple of years ago, I saw this dear lady for the first time since that Bible study. When she saw me, the first words out of her mouth were, "Rachel, you saved my life." She proceeded to tell me that Operation Kill Crappy Art had been successful and she would never forget how thankful she was that I was willing to tell her about my similar experience.

I had forgotten all about sharing that tip with her. And I could never have dreamed that God would use that incredibly overwhelming experience to help someone else in distress.

The Lord works in mysterious ways.

～ ～ ～

Pillars of Truth to Lean On

When I need to overcome the overwhelming, I rely on these beautiful passages for strength.

- The LORD is my strength and my shield; in him my heart trusts, and I am helped; my heart exults, and with my song I give thanks to him. (Psalm 28:7)
- From the end of the earth I call to you when my heart is faint. Lead me to the rock that is higher than I. (Psalm 61:2)
- When my spirit faints within me, you know my way! In the path where I walk they have hidden a trap for me. (Psalm 142:3)
- Be strong in the Lord and in the strength of his might. (Ephesians 6:10)

Stepping Stone #8

The last thing you need when you are overwhelmed is another to-do item on your list. Stepping Stone #8 is to write down four items *not* to do when you are overwhelmed. For example, I don't add any more items to my to-do list unless an item is removed. I purposely slow down and don't jump into anything new quickly. I refuse to miss my daily quiet time with God. These are just a few of my things not to do when feeling overwhelmed. Take your four items and write them into a prayer to God, knowing that your steps are established by him. Choose one of the tips from this chapter for your focus tip and write down your answers to the questions following the tip in your *One More Step* journal.

nine

Ditch Your Carry-on

I woke, the dungeon flamed with light;
my chains fell off, my heart was free.

—Charles Wesley

Becoming a mom to a special-needs child expanded my world like never before. I wouldn't have guessed how many people spoke harsh words over those with special needs or purposely neglected to help those with extra physical or mental requirements. The Sunday school teacher who thought I didn't want to help my child was only the first to openly criticize my parenting skills. I truthfully would never have dreamed that people of all ages and stages could fail miserably to give grace to a little girl with a disease she never requested. But they did.

One particular incident happened at school in the early years of Taylor's developmental issues. At this stage of her disease, she was extremely hyper and flitted from activity to activity with little focus. Daily life was a huge safety challenge. At the time, I was working a full-time office job, and each day after preschool, a baby-sitter would pick up Taylor from school and care for her for a few hours. When the baby-sitter stopped by the school to get Taylor, the teacher said, "Good luck with her today."

When the baby-sitter shared with me the teacher's remark, it stung. I understood her frustration and personal limit of patience, but that teacher held college degrees as a specialist in early childhood education. She was supposed to be a professional!

When Taylor was a little older but still quite the busy girl, we encountered an issue in the grocery store. Matt and I had nicknamed her Elastigirl because her hands were unbelievably quick. While we laughed about her grabbing habit at home and guarded plates of food any time we walked past her, others didn't understand her requirement for personal space.

One day as I shopped for groceries, Taylor sat in the shopping cart seat. I talked to her to keep her busy and attached toys to the cart handle in order to keep her little fingers occupied. While I turned away to find a particular item from the shelf, a woman pulled her shopping cart right next to Taylor and left it there while she walked down the aisle. Taylor's quick instinct kicked in, and she grabbed the loaf of bread from the top of the woman's cart. Before I knew what had happened, the woman began to scold Taylor.

"Why did you do that?" she said. "Don't you know any better?" When I heard the woman's hateful tone, I turned toward her, in shock that she had the audacity to scold Taylor. I could feel the rage boiling inside me, but somehow managed not to return her scream. I looked at the woman with both disgust and pity. Though I remained calm externally, the words I chose to hurl back at her are not ones I typically choose now, nor should I type them out in this book. Like winter hibernation had just ended, the mother bear in me broke out.

The problem with all these comments and negative situations was that I carried them around like baggage. They followed me and haunted me and flat out made me angry. When others made poor decisions, many times due to ignorance over Taylor's behavior, I harbored bitterness in my heart and sometimes lashed back at their words or actions.

For a couple of years, I struggled over dealing with these types of negative scenarios. I felt justified in my responses, and sometimes I was. At times I wished I could have an "easy life like they did." But I didn't realize all the dead weight I carried from resentment.

Job's Prayer of Forgiveness

When I ask folks on my blog or in social media settings, "Who is your favorite Bible character?" someone will always mention Job. In a nutshell, his story begins with a conversation between God and Satan. God asks Satan, "Have you seen my main man, Job, recently?" To which Satan says, "Of course I've seen him. No wonder he obeys you—you've given him everything he needs and more."

God allows Satan to test Job, and, wow, does Satan get busy on it! The next thing we know, Job has lost all his children and all his wealth. His wife's advice is to curse God and die, and his friends are not much of an encouragement either. In all this, Job still worships God, so Satan decides to pull the last straw. He asks God for permission to give Job physical issues, and God allows it. Then Satan curses Job with boils over his entire body. Job himself is seized with his own humanity and wishes he had never been born.

While Job sits in ashes, scraping the boils, the debates begin between Job and his "friends." I prefer to call Job's friends "frenemies," but I'm not sure that was a word in the original Hebrew text, so we'll stick with "friends." After Job and his "friends" finish their hot discussion, Job feels like he just can't take one more step, and he wants to give up. He even curses the day he was born.

Then God comes to Job and speaks through a whirlwind. "Where were you when I laid the foundation of the earth? . . . Who shut in the sea with doors when it burst out from the womb? . . . Can you lift up your voice to the clouds, that a flood of waters may cover you? . . . Who has

put wisdom in the inward parts or given understanding to the mind? . . .
Is it at your command that the eagle mounts up and makes his nest on
high?" (Job 38:4, 8, 34, 36; 39:27).

When the Lord finishes questioning him, Job immediately repents.
God then turns his attention to Job's friends and requires them to make
sacrifices to atone for the sin of speaking falsely, in their own prideful
knowledge, against Job.

Recently I read every detail of this story until the final chapter. When
I arrived at 42:10, my heart paused: "The LORD restored the fortunes of
Job, when he had prayed for his friends. And the LORD gave Job twice as
much as he had before."

God restored Job beyond his original prosperity, making him twice
as wealthy as he was before, but the Bible says this occurred "when he had
prayed for his friends."

I don't know about you, but I'm not sure I would have easily forgiven
my "friends." They let me down when I needed them the most. They crit-
icized me at my lowest point. They not only offered no support, but they
tore me apart. Job could have felt this way. And maybe he did initially. We
don't know for sure. But whatever heart issues Job may have felt about the
advice of his friends and family, he knew where to take the problem. Job
went to God in prayer when no one else understood what was happening
to him. He released the dead weight by forgiving his friends.

Forgiving others doesn't mean we agree with their attitudes or sins
against us. No one "deserves" forgiveness for wrongdoing. As Christians,
we don't forgive because someone deserves to be forgiven. As C. S. Lewis
states, "To be a Christian means to forgive the inexcusable, because God
has forgiven the inexcusable in you."[3]

We forgive because God forgave us. Paul reminds us to put on compassionate hearts, "bearing with one another and, if one has a complaint

against another, forgiving each other; as the Lord has forgiven you, so you also must forgive" (Colossians 3:13).

When our friends have let us down, we are tempted to hold their failure over their heads. When our family members attempt to help but their words feel more hurtful than anything, we tend to withdraw and hold a grudge. This is the natural human response. I've been there time and time again. I especially remember all the grudges I held against those who wrongly responded to Taylor's special needs.

Our reaction to being wronged is to offer resentment and rejection. God's response to being wronged is to offer resolution and restoration. We have the choice to react as humans or to respond as God would. Paul explains it like this:

> Therefore, if anyone is in Christ, he is a new creation. The old has passed away; behold, the new has come. All this is from God, who through Christ reconciled us to himself and gave us the ministry of reconciliation; that is, in Christ God was reconciling the world to himself, not counting their trespasses against them, and entrusting to us the message of reconciliation. (2 Corinthians 5:17–19)

We may think we are simply not making the choice to forgive. But we *are* making a choice. Instead of choosing to reconcile, we are choosing to resent.

Resentment comes in varying degrees, according to the level of emotion we feel about the issue. Maybe we will just "not talk" to the person. We draw lines of how far we will interact with this friend or family member because of her insulting conversation or behavior toward us. When we hold on to the resentment long enough, then resentment often results in rejection. We simply stop all communication and close off the relationship.

When Adam and Eve first chose to sin, God planned to resolve conflicts and restore relationships. Though the consequences of Adam and Eve's choice reverberated down through generations, God wanted to resume the intimate relationship he had enjoyed with them in the Garden of Eden. He created a means of atoning for sin through the sacrifices of animals and planned for the world's redemption through the ultimate sacrifice of his Son.

When we choose to forgive, we follow Christ's example and honor God. Once we've made the choice to forgive, we can work on resolving our attitude regarding the person and situation. The goal is a renewed relationship. When we resolve our attitude by giving the problem to God, we take one more step toward restoration.

In the graph below, we can see the progression of steps for God's response and our natural response and where each can lead us.

Human Reaction	Godly Response
Resentment	Resolution
▼	▼
Rejection	Restoration
▼	▼
Relationship Destruction	Renewal

I believe that as Christians we hold grudges because we forget just how much we have been forgiven. God's love sent his Son to die on the cross for us! While sometimes we fail to remember God's love for us, we also sometimes fail to remember his forgiveness of our sins.

We know that we need to forgive; we can see it. But seeing it is so much easier than doing it.

Solomon's Prayer on Forgiveness

In 1 Kings 8:23, Solomon begins a prayer of dedication of the first house of God. He beautifully and eloquently praises God for the opportunity to build the temple. He honors the Lord in this prayer through his acknowledgment that God is far bigger than a building. Specifically, he states that while God expands beyond the universe, he willingly and lovingly meets with his people in the temple. He requests that the Lord will hear his people when they pray in his house, and he repeats this request through the remaining verses in chapter 8.

But then in verse 39 he offers an unusual request: "Then hear in heaven your dwelling place and forgive and act and render to each whose heart you know, according to all his ways (for you, you only, know the hearts of all the children of mankind)."

The wisest man to live asks the Lord to make decisions according to the hearts of those who request. He acknowledges that God alone knows the hearts. I find it interesting that this section is in parentheses. It's as if Solomon is saying these words in a sidebar, but just in case anyone should ever be confused about this topic, he's throwing them in.

Only God knows if the words of your relative were intended to hurt you or if they slipped out unintentionally. Only God knows if that friend premeditated her actions or just responded in a human act of rashness. Only God knows if you are harboring bitterness because you don't want to forgive someone who truly wronged you. Only God knows the heart.

So I can't judge my husband, or my sister, or my brother, or my daughter, or my friend, or anyone else. If I'm having a hard time forgiving someone for his words or actions and I'm feeling weighed down, unable to step forward, then I need to ask myself:

- Am I chasing after dreams and goals but feeling burdened and unable to run?
- Am I using up strength by carrying the extra weight of resentment?
- Does the weight of my burden stem from an unforgiving heart?

The choice to forgive is a choice to live. Maybe today is the day you've been waiting for: the day you find strength because you make the choice to forgive. In choosing to overlook the wrong, you refuse to harbor bitterness and by doing so experience the freedom that forgiveness offers.

Christ's Prayer of Forgiveness

If you're saying, "But you don't know what I've been through," then you're right. I don't know the depths of hurt you've endured. I don't know who or where or how. But I do know that no matter how difficult the situation, the tighter our grip on harmful feelings, the heavier our burdens. The more we hold on to an unforgiving spirit, the more difficult it is to take another step forward.

My mind can't fully conceive the crucifixion of Christ. While Jesus carried the weight of the world's sin, the anguish he endured on every level was beyond excruciating. As he carried the cross up Calvary's hill, the hope of the world rested on his shoulders as the weight of the cross wrenched his body. Each time his foot moved forward, the pain ripped through his muscles. Then his hands and feet were nailed to that cross, and the soldiers plunged it into the ground. Pushing himself up for every breath, Christ suffered excruciating pain, whether inhaling or exhaling.

Physically, emotionally, mentally, and spiritually, the depth of sorrow he experienced in this moment is unimaginable. Yet even as he hung on the cross, he asked his Father in heaven, "Father, forgive them, for they know not what they do" (Luke 23:34).

As he endured the torture of the cross and the suffering of separation from his Father, Jesus requested forgiveness on behalf of those who needed it. Even as his body was racked with pain and his spirit endured crushing blows, his response was to extend grace. As a result of his choice, the sin problem for the entire world was resolved. Humankind has the opportunity to be restored into full relationship with the Creator of the universe. Each individual can experience a renewed mind, soul, and spirit, and someday in heaven, a renewed body.

My Prayer of Forgiveness

During those early years after obtaining Taylor's diagnosis of MPS, harboring bitterness became a pastime for me. The people who often frustrated me the most were Christians—shouldn't they know how to respond positively to negative situations? Yet I knew my struggle was as real as theirs. Even some of my own decisions seemed unforgivable, and I found myself in a cycle of reacting, resenting, and rejecting.

Thankfully, Matt and I were privileged to be part of an incredible worship ministry in our church. Each week, I played the keyboard and Matt sang with the choir or praise team. Our godly worship pastor knew the intense struggles we faced. What he didn't know was the unforgiving burden I carried in my heart. As we began rehearsal one Wednesday night, the Holy Spirit carried a powerful message through the words to an anthem of blessing God's name. As the words of praise described God's forgiveness, I felt the conviction in my heart.

How could I stand and praise the Lord who forgave me when I refused to forgive others for the stockpile of hurtful situations I had endured? That night the tears flowed as I played the keyboard and listened to the choir sing the lyrics. I ditched the carry-on luggage I'd carried in my heart for so long by letting go of unforgiving feelings. I made the choice to forgive those who had hurt me, both the ones who knew they hurt me and those who had no idea of the pain they had caused. What a huge relief I felt from the burden I had been carrying for so long! For the first time in years, the heavy weight of resentment was gone—all because I chose to give it to the Lord and simply forgive. I still had to address certain situations and would continue to deal with circumstances resulting from mistakes of others, but the resentment problem within my heart was resolved.

Learning to forgive others is a process, isn't it? If only we needed to issue forgiveness just one time. If only people didn't continually make mistakes and hurts weren't endured over and over, perhaps forgiving would come a little easier to us. **If only we freely forgave with as much strength as we grip grudges.**

God forgives us not only for our past sin but also for daily mistakes. As we aspire to follow his steps, we will discover that by forgiving others, we find strength for one more step in the journey.

～ ～ ～

Pillars of Truth to Lean On

When forgiving seems difficult, read the following verses to remember how wonderful it is to be forgiven.

- For you, O Lord, are good and forgiving, abounding in steadfast love to all who call upon you. (Psalm 86:5)
- Whenever you stand praying, forgive, if you have anything against anyone, so that your Father also who is in heaven may forgive you your trespasses. (Mark 11:25)
- Judge not, and you will not be judged; condemn not, and you will not be condemned; forgive, and you will be forgiven. (Luke 6:37)
- Finally, brothers, rejoice. Aim for restoration, comfort one another, agree with one another, live in peace; and the God of love and peace will be with you. (2 Corinthians 13:11)
- Be kind to one another, tenderhearted, forgiving one another, as God in Christ forgave you. (Ephesians 4:32)

Stepping Stone #9

Forgiveness is a gift we both give and receive. Take a moment to pray and ask God to forgive you for any grudges you've gripped tightly. Repent of your refusal to forgive others, even though he graciously has forgiven you. Release your burden to him and then write out your prayer of requesting forgiveness. Write down the name of someone(s) who needs your forgiveness today and include her in your *One More Step* journal entry. Now you can anticipate the freedom that results in forgiveness—praise Jesus!

ten

Stop Watering the Weeds

And while the wave-notes fall on my ear,
everything false will disappear.

—Clara H. Scott

When you live with someone who has been medically assigned a number of years, at times your thoughts start to merge together in strange ways. The grief process, which begins the moment you comprehend your loved one has a terminal illness, can include many stages and phases. Some people go through a denial period. Some postpone the reality in their minds because "plenty of time" is left. For some the process lasts longer than others. No rules exist. Just feelings. And life. And God.

After the birthing experience with Taylor, when pregnancy hormones kicked in with my other babies, my mind would swirl with worry and anxiety. *What if the baby is sick? What if my water breaks and I need an emergency C-section again? Why is God giving us another child? We can barely meet the needs of the ones we have. What if something happens to Taylor while I'm pregnant? She'll never know this sibling, and he or she will never have the privilege of getting to know her.*

On the upswing of the hormones, I knew that each child was a unique gift to our family as we steadily grew from a blended family of four to ultimately a large family of nine. I knew God would take care of us and help us no matter what we went through. I had no doubt that his plan and purpose were far beyond my mind's comprehension, and all peace came from him. But oh, the mental roller coaster!

Mind battles are vicious and demand attention. For me, the winter season seems to exacerbate the cycles of negative thoughts. One winter seemed particularly long, and I remember how the fresh breath of spring smelled delicious when it finally arrived. On a warmer afternoon in the beginning of that spring, our family worked in the backyard to encourage new growth. Each child had a job watering or weeding or gathering or mulching.

My seven-year-old son had grown tired of weeding and needed a little less work intensity, so he took a turn at watering. Though all the weeds had not been pulled, he happily began to water each baby plant we had nestled in the ground. But he wasn't all that careful in his watering, and I found myself saying, "Don't water the weeds, buddy."

In that moment, I realized: *Oh my word, this is what I do—I water the weeds of my mind!*

Have you been there? The feeling of wanting to give up begins with one thought, and before you know it, the thoughts have escalated to the point of negative entrapment. You didn't intend to zap your own strength, but somewhere along the line, you allowed yourself to make poor thought choices, which in turn led to poor decisions. Pretty soon you are saying to yourself, *I give up!*

When I spend hours either alone or caring for children without any adult conversation, my mind can easily get trapped in negative self-talk and I begin to think:

What if it doesn't work out?

How will we ever be able to accomplish that?

I wonder if she thinks I'm . . .

In a day's time, I've had more conversations with myself than I ever care to admit. I could be cleaning the toilets, but am I thinking about toilets? No. I could be cooking dinner, but am I thinking about dinner? Not necessarily.

Occasionally negative internal chatter carries over to a conversation with my husband, and sometimes his response is, "Where did that come from?"

Just like a flushed toilet spiraling downward, my mind, at times, follows a similar trend. As with any habit in need of change, I had to learn not only to discontinue the negative internal chatter but also to replace it.

In the midst of depression, grief, or fighting any battle of the mind, no one wants to be told, "Think positive thoughts." We all know it's important to think positively. But how do we do it? We have to purposefully set our minds on truth. Thinking positively often requires digging deep and making choices that are contrary to our feelings.

Replacing Negativity with Truthful Thoughts

In Philippians 4:8, Paul tells us exactly what we should think about:

> Whatsoever things are true, whatsoever things are honest, whatsoever things are just, whatsoever things are pure, whatsoever things are lovely, whatsoever things are of good report; if there be any virtue, and if there be any praise, think on these things. (KJV)

To discover the key to replacing negative internal chatter, I began to dwell on applicable thoughts of truth. Whether the issue is self-confidence, anger, worry, or anxiety, *truth* must be our guide to replacing the negative internal chatter that so often feeds the emotion of wanting to give up. Consider the following examples of my truth exchange.

My feeling: I feel like things are out of control!

The truth: God is in control.

The proof: "Many are the plans in the mind of a man, but it is the purpose of the LORD that will stand" (Proverbs 19:21).

The point: Though I may not feel like it in the moment, God reigns over every detail of his plans.

My feeling: This issue is driving me crazy!

The truth: God can make something good from this.

The proof: "We know that for those who love God all things work together for good, for those who are called according to his purpose" (Romans 8:28).

The point: While I may not enjoy this circumstance, God can take anything and use it for my good and his glory.

My feeling: This problem seems too small to ask for help. I'm such a wimp.

The truth: We serve a God who loves to work through the details.

The proof: "If God so clothes the grass, which is alive in the field today, and tomorrow is thrown into the oven, how much more will he clothe you, O you of little faith!" (Luke 12:28).

The point: While I think this issue seems like one I should be able to handle on my own, God pursues the smallest of details.

My feeling: I feel like they deserve to be paid back for what they did.

The truth: God will issue justice.

The proof: "Do not say, 'I will repay evil'; wait for the LORD, and he will deliver you" (Proverbs 20:22).

The point: When I want to take matters into my own hands, God's got this.

By trading the negative self-talk for the truth of God's Word, I discovered the secret to combating negative internal chatter. For every negative thought, I checked myself and substituted God's promises. Through this exchange, I gained clarity of mind and a positive focus. What a wonderful feeling to think clearly and anticipate God's work in the midst of daily routine!

Replacing Negativity with Honorable Thoughts

I read Philippians 4:8 in various Bible versions, and two other words were used in place of "honorable": *honest* and *noble.* As I dug deeper, I discovered the original Greek word translated "honorable" indicates "to hold in deep respect." Paul is telling us to think honorable thoughts—thoughts that are respectful of God, others, and *ourselves.* We are to think not only on things that are true but also on things that offer dignity to our life status.

If we have accepted Jesus as our Savior, we are God's children, heirs to the throne of heaven (see Titus 3:7). In reflecting on Paul's charge to think on things that are honorable, I believe he wants us to think like the child of the King, as the princesses we are.

That negative internal chatter is *not* very princess-like. This is the reason it is important to turn off the negative internal chatter and reflect on things that are reverential—because we want to reflect the glory the King deserves.

Replacing Negativity with Just Thoughts

Most of us would probably think of the following words in connection to the word *just: justice, righteousness,* and *fairness.* All of those would be great choices of how our thoughts should line up against negativity. Am I thinking fairly? Would God consider this thought to be righteous?

Wrong thoughts are not just. Negative thoughts are not just. No question about it.

When I studied this verse, I found that the Greek definition for the word *just* in this particular verse means "righteous." So we were correct in our connections above. But I was drawn in when I looked at the entire definition:

Just: righteous, observing God's laws

So many times, negative internal chatter stems from one little difference between our thinking and the above definition: we are focused on human laws and not God's laws. We think in terms of right and wrong according to our human minds. This thought process can cause the weeds of negative internal chatter to grow like nothing else. We allow the comparison game to take hold . . . and I know you get what I'm talking about here.

- *I wish he would just do the right thing and stop _____ (fill in the blank).*
- *She knows that is not what the Bible says. She really needs to get right with God.*
- *Why aren't my children behaving as well as theirs?*
- *Why aren't their children behaving as well as mine?*

Focusing on the rules and regulations created by humans can flip the switch of inside negative chatter. In order to put a stop to it, we must stop focusing on what others say is right and wrong. According to Paul, "When they measure themselves by one another and compare themselves with one another, they are without understanding" (2 Corinthians 10:12).

When Paul tells us in Philippians 4:8 to think on "just" things, he is directing us to a focal point of God's—not human—laws. And what are God's laws?

When Jesus was asked about the greatest commandments, he boiled it down to two simple laws of God: "'You shall love the Lord your God with all your heart and with all your soul and with all your mind and with all your strength.' The second is this: 'You shall love your neighbor as yourself.' There is no other commandment greater than these" (Mark 12:30–31).

True justice is obeying God's laws, not merely observing human laws. We can stop negative internal chatter when we simply love God and love others because this is true justice. When we choose not to judge others according to their actions but according to how God wants us to care for them, unfavorable thoughts don't have the chance to enter our minds. If we love people regardless of their religious beliefs, ethnicity, or status, we won't think poorly of them.

Replacing Negativity with Pure Thoughts

As I read through multiple translations of Philippians 4:8, I noticed that while many of the words differ slightly from translation to translation, the word *pure* is the same for every translation.

According to Dictionary.com, *pure* means "free from extraneous matter." In church culture today, we've used the word *pure* so often in regard to sexual matters that I believe we immediately think, *Paul is telling us to clean up our thought lives from a sexual perspective.*

But when I view the definitions of *pure* and I focus on the original language in which the verse was written, I have to believe that sexual issues were not all that Paul intended for us to focus on with regard to remaining pure.

Purity in our thought lives includes keeping our minds from thinking *anything* that shouldn't be there. I'll be honest, this is a tough one for me. How can I, born a sinner, think only pure thoughts? This seems impossible! But I continually reflect on Psalm 119:9, where the psalmist provides clear direction for how we can remain pure in our thoughts and deeds. He writes, "How can a young man keep his way pure? By guarding it according to your word."

When we fix our minds on the Word of God, negative internal chatter will dissipate, evaporate, vanish in midair. **God's Word is the key to turning negative internal chatter into a disappearing act.**

The current "cool" thing to do is to add flavor to your water. The stores offer many types and brands of water flavoring. I suppose that's okay. But I don't like anything extra in my water. Not dirt, not rocks, not impurities, not lemon, not even flavoring. I still enjoy my water on a simple level—pure with nothing extra added.

Perhaps the next time you feel yourself turning into a negative internal chatter maniac, you could drink a cup of cold water. And while you're drinking it, ask the Father in Jesus's name to make your heart just like that water—pure with nothing extra added.

Replacing Negativity with Thoughts of Good Report

Being intentional about our thought lives is a critical element to crushing negative internal chatter. And Paul says we're supposed to think on things of "good report." The English Standard Version uses the word *commendable.* Because I'm a word freak, I love researching the various translations and words to help me understand the meaning of the original language. When I drilled down into the meaning of a "good report," using *Thayer's Greek Lexicon,* I read, "Things spoken in a kindly spirit, with good-will to others."[4]

You see, we take that one negative sentence someone said and we replay it in our minds over and over. Pretty soon, the significance of the statement grows to epic proportions, overpowering the multitude of good reports.

You remember only the college teacher who gave you a B when it should have been an A, even though you got only one B the entire year.

You focus on the girl who remarked that the dessert you made for the tea could have been better if you had added more sugar, though forty other people complimented its beauty and delicious flavor.

You obsess over the coworker who felt you could have improved your presentation if you'd only spent a few more minutes tweaking it, despite the fact that your boss knew you deserved the promotion as a result of that very presentation.

I believe Paul is telling me to take all the book reviews on Amazon and focus on the positive ones. And use all the sweet e-mails from readers to fan the flame of my love of writing. And place all those kind social media messages on the replay button of my mind. The things spoken in a kindly spirit with goodwill. That's one translation for me.

Paul calls us to treat the one teeny tiny negative statement in a sea of good reports as the speck of sand that it is. But what does this mean for you? Maybe it means remembering why you married your husband when his words get a bit jumbled. Perhaps it means focusing on that one positive obedient action from your child for the day. Or it could mean reflecting on the sweet smile of the barista before she spilled your coffee this morning. Or the time God gave you to pray while you waited in traffic for forty-five minutes.

Replacing Negativity with Praiseworthy Thoughts

As if the other items on the list aren't enough, Paul adds this "little" idea that we are to think on things that are praiseworthy. In my mind, it's easy to look at this list and think that Paul had an order. First, whatever is true. Then whatever is honorable . . . and the list builds sequentially. Or it may seem like this is our check-off list of criteria.

While I have no proof to confirm my philosophy on Paul's recommended list, I feel like he was saying, "If your thoughts meet any one topic of this list, you're in good shape. And this last one of praise is icing on the cake!" Matthew Henry, the great Bible commentary author, mentions that this word *praise* means "worthy of commendation." When I think about the One who is worthy, the praise swells in my heart, and my spirit is lifted. When I praise Jesus, I feel incapable of concentrating on anything else, and that praise then carries me through the times when Satan whispers, *It's time to give up.*

Praising Jesus overpowers potential negativity! Satan will *not* hang around where Jesus is being praised, so if your desire is to stop the negative internal chatter, then praising God is the most powerful weapon in your arsenal.

How Does Your Garden Grow?

Our minds are like gardens. We cultivate our thoughts, either accidentally or purposefully. My son had no idea that watering the weeds was the wrong thing to do. But his example caused me to realize that I often cultivate negative thoughts without realizing it. With strong effort, I have found four deliberate choices that stop negative self-talk dead in its tracks and purposefully replace it with beautiful thoughts.

1. Pull out the self-cultivated weeds.

When tough circumstances come into our lives, it is easy to generate negative thoughts associated with the circumstances. After all, life's not fair. Many times I've wished, even demanded, that God change the situation. I've felt that no one listened or cared. I've felt that others just didn't get it. But my experience has been that the more I've attempted to justify those weeds, the bigger they grew. The more I repeated those thoughts, the stronger their roots became. So I've learned the best thing we can do to self-pity is pull out that bad weed before it has a chance to grow. When the thought initially presents itself, zap it swiftly.

Baby step: Make a list of recurring thoughts that you know need to be zapped as soon as they creep in.

2. Don't water the weeds.

Okay, so we zapped as many recurring self-cultivated thoughts as we could, but we know that those negative thoughts still affect our minds through the influences we choose. Jesus explained it this way: "The eye is the lamp of the body. So, if your eye is healthy, your whole body will be full of light, but if your eye is bad, your whole body will be full of darkness. If then the light in you is darkness, how great is the darkness!" (Matthew 6:22–23).

If the gates of the mind, the eyes, are taking in negativity, then the mind is required to decide how to process that negative information. Isn't it a better choice to guard the gates of the mind and choose not to look at those things that would cause the weeds to be the highest plants in the garden?

A common example of "watering the weeds" is allowing negative social media content to stream in our feeds. If someone you know fills every social media post with foul language or nonstop complaining, then the best choice is not to water those weeds.

Baby step: Carefully analyze your mental influences, including, but not limited to, social media, television, entertainment, books, games, media of all types, etc. Purposely choose to block negative influences out of your mind's gate.

3. Plant the seeds.

In order to grow a strong garden, we must place the seeds in the ground and cover them with soil. Then, little by little, the roots grow deeper and deeper. The replacement thoughts outlined in this chapter can be planted by reading and memorizing God's Word. The more Scripture we read and memorize, the more the healthy, positive plants can grow. Some of my favorite seeds are mentioned in Philippians 4:8; Proverbs 19:21; Mark 12:30; and Romans 8:28.

Baby step: Memorize Philippians 4:8 by reading it every day for a week, writing it down each time you read it. (For more resources on memorizing Scripture, check out http://rachelwojo.com/bible-memory -verse/.)

4. Fertilize with the Miracle-Gro of gratitude.

Gratitude will fertilize a strong mind; showing our thanks will cultivate serious growth. Paul advises us to "give thanks in all circumstances; for this is the will of God in Christ Jesus for you" (1 Thessalonians 5:18).

I'm thankful that this verse states "give thanks in." Because there are things *for* which I struggle to be thankful. It's hard to be thankful for a broken toe. It's difficult to be thankful for an empty bank account. It's tough to be thankful for a broken dishwasher. But I can be thankful *in* the circumstance because there is always *something* to be thankful for. I can be thankful for medical treatment for the broken toe. I can be thankful for an opportunity to earn money for the bank account. I can be thankful for dirty dishes because that means I ate a meal. Find what you can be thankful for and dwell on it. I've found making lists of things for which I'm thankful is a wonderful way to fertilize strong thought processes in my mind.

Baby step: Make a list of things for which you are thankful. Repeat this step no less than weekly.

How do I explain living each day with the knowledge that my child has a terminal disease and her life on earth is limited? If I dwell on this fact alone, the negative mental chatter produces weeds at a massive rate. So I stopped watering the weeds. While I haven't become a master gardener quite yet, I can tell you that when I follow the proper gardening steps, the negative internal chatter is minimal and the mental garden results are beautiful. Lush green plants of faith and trust grow freely. Flowers of hope and joy flourish. Blossoms of love abound.

～ ～ ～

Pillars of Truth to Lean On

To stop negative internal chatter before it takes over, use these verses to fertilize a healthy mind.

- Many are the plans in the mind of a man, but it is the purpose of the LORD that will stand. (Proverbs 19:21)
- You keep him in perfect peace whose mind is stayed on you, because he trusts in you. (Isaiah 26:3)
- To set the mind on the flesh is death, but to set the mind on the Spirit is life and peace. (Romans 8:6)
- We know that for those who love God all things work together for good, for those who are called according to his purpose. (Romans 8:28)

Stepping Stone #10

When we permit negative thoughts to escalate, everything that flows from our hearts is negative. In order to take those thoughts captive (see 2 Corinthians 10:5), choose one of the replacement thoughts we discovered from Paul and write it out by filling in the blanks of the following statement in your *One More Step* journal:

"Instead of dwelling on the negative thought of _____, I am choosing to think purposefully on _____."

Write down a list of ten items for which you are thankful and praise God for them in prayer. Way to go! He sees your progress and is with you every step of the way!

eleven

Fighting Fatigue

*Against the foe in vales below let all our
strength be hurled.*

—John H. Yates

We didn't agree on absolutely everything, but still we were best friends. The stereotypical tense relationship of mother and teenage daughter never existed between my mom and me. And in my first wedding at age twenty-one, I begged her to be my matron of honor.

"Don't you want one of your young, pretty friends to stand with you?" she asked.

"No, Mom. I want you. You're my best friend and I want you to be there."

It took some convincing, but she finally agreed.

When Taylor's father and I separated, Mom thought I might return home to live, but I chose to keep my job and provide for Taylor the best I could. We visited each other often, in spite of the five-hour drive, and while I knew Mom wasn't feeling well, I didn't realize how sick she was. Each time I saw her throughout that fall, she appeared weaker. Nonetheless, she picked garden vegetables and canned homemade grape juice as she had done for as long as I could remember, so I convinced myself it was nothing severe. She looked weak but continued to push through her daily tasks.

At the end of the year, after Mom finally saw a specialist, she was diagnosed with a rare type of anemia. Anemia couldn't be all that bad, right? I mean, growing up, my sisters and I had been slightly anemic. We took extra iron and dealt with the occasional bloody nose that occurred for no reason. So I wasn't too worried.

By the next month, Mom was even weaker. I continued to brush it off until the day my sister called with news that I could no longer ignore. My heart sank and I could barely hold the phone to my ear as I heard her say that Mom's diagnosis had been changed. I couldn't hold back the sobs until my sister and I finished the conversation. Mom didn't have anemia. She had leukemia. Quite the world of difference.

Mom began to grow more and more tired. Her weakness could be alleviated only by blood transfusions. And after a few weeks, even blood transfusions couldn't buy time. Her body could no longer process the transfusions. As she grew weaker, she made every effort to sit up when visitors dropped by. She did her best to make eye contact with each person present in the room and fought fatigue until her body would no longer cooperate.

Six months after Mom's leukemia diagnosis, my dad, my eight siblings, and I gathered to say a temporary good-bye to Mom. The loss I felt on the day we buried her consumes my spirit even as I share this story more than fourteen years later. I can't help but weep as I type. My mom was the best Christian I have ever known. I am so blessed that from the moment I was born, she taught me that being tired is never a reason to give up.

I know you've been there: sometimes we feel like quitting because we are simply too tired to keep going. Unable to listen to even one more piece of encouraging advice, we shut down. Incapable of taking just one more step, we stop moving altogether. Even small breaths of air feel suffocating, and suddenly we can't go on.

What can we do when fatigue saturates us, body, soul, and spirit?

In Exodus 17, we find the children of Israel taking the initial steps of their forty-year journey of wandering through the wilderness. Talk about exhaustion! Can you imagine how tiring that was? Recently I took a mission trip, and due to poor weather, we missed our connecting flight. We were rerouted, which resulted in a thirty-two-hour travel time to reach our destination. After barely sleeping for almost three days, I could hardly speak. I learned one important lesson: traveling results in fatigue. And, wow, the children of Israel were traveling!

After the Israelites waved good-bye to the few sea bubbles remaining of the Egyptians, they resorted to the comfort of complaining. "Moses, we need water. What are we going to do? Did you bring us out here to die?"

Moses took the matter before the Lord. God told Moses to hit the rock with his staff and God would provide the water. Moses obeyed and the children of Israel witnessed yet another miracle. Ah, such a sweet story.

But.

But then they entered the first battle since fleeing Egypt. The Amalekites—ruthless warriors—went out to fight Israel. The Bible refers to their fierceness in the following passage:

> Remember what Amalek did to you on the way as you came out
> of Egypt, how he attacked you on the way *when you were faint
> and weary,* and cut off your tail, those who were lagging behind
> you, and he did not fear God. Therefore when the LORD your
> God has given you rest from all your enemies around you, in the
> land that the LORD your God is giving you for an inheritance to
> possess, you shall blot out the memory of Amalek from under
> heaven; you shall not forget. (Deuteronomy 25:17–19)

When did the Amalekites attack Israel? *When they were faint and weary.*

It seems that with the miracles they had witnessed God perform, this mighty group of people who had survived being overworked as slaves would not have grown tired. But the Israelites had to learn to rely on the only true Source of strength, the Lord God. I don't know about you, but I've found that when I'm "faint and weary," many times it is because I've been relying on my own strength instead of looking to the Lord to sustain and restore me.

Before the Israelites began to fight the battle with the Amalekites, they were fighting the battle of exhaustion. They were physically tired of traveling in the wilderness, sleeping in tents with zero luxuries, and searching for food and water. They were mentally tired of trying to figure out the next step forward. They must have held many campfire conversations about which way they should be going. They were emotionally tired from the highs and lows of experiencing slavery and then freedom. They were spiritually tired of trying to comprehend God's plan for the nation.

The Israelites have something to teach as well: we also battle the same types of fatigue—physical, mental, emotional, and spiritual.

Fighting Physical Fatigue

If we're honest, we all get tired because, well, we are human. God created our bodies with limitations. But God also designed our bodies with purpose and order. When we sleep, eat, and exercise in daily routine, our bodies carry rhythm, and God's intended order for our bodies is fulfilled.

Divine design outlined visual cues for us regarding the issue of rest. God called them day and night. While there are many exceptions that interfere with rest patterns, such as shift work, sleep disorders, and more, when we maintain sleep-promoting habits, our bodies are more apt to rest well.

Examples of sleep-promoting habits might include going to bed at the same time each night, avoiding food or any stimulants before bedtime, praying before trying to fall asleep, and reading Scripture or books. In order to prevent physical fatigue from shutting down our bodies or zapping all our energy, we must find a physical rhythm of obtaining rest.

Choosing to rest is not always a popular decision, but it is a wise one.

Things can get pretty wild at our house. With six kids under one roof, rest is hard to find. The physical and mental demands are high. But I've found that when the children have regular bedtimes and Matt and I have regularly scheduled downtime to enjoy each other, our busy lives are much easier to manage.

Managing chaos requires more energy than maintaining rhythm. I encourage you to find a rhythm to your daily habits of sleeping, eating, and exercise. Yes, you will need to be flexible along the way. Yes, things will happen to get you off track. But maintaining a daily life rhythm can definitely help to prevent fatigue. By sleeping a regular number of hours each night, your body refuels itself. Maintaining this regular rest cycle will promote continual refreshment and prevent burnout.

Baby step: Choose one sleep-promoting habit from the examples above and try it for seven days.

Fighting Mental Fatigue

Sometimes when I say I am tired, I mean that my brain is tired and I'm struggling for clarity and creativity due to mental fatigue. Using brain power requires strength. If your job demands mental acuity much of the workday, you may feel as if you have done nothing physical the entire day, yet you have no energy. Perhaps you are doing some physical activity, but you spend the majority of your day using mental energy. Or maybe your physical fatigue has carried over to other areas and you find yourself mentally tired due to physical exhaustion.

When I find myself tiring mentally, I take breaks by doing a routine physical activity that requires almost no thinking. I'll stand at the kitchen sink and wash dishes or run down to the basement and throw in a load of laundry. I've also found that if I don't waste mental energy on digital devices, I have more mental energy to do the things I truly need to accomplish.

If I'm struggling for both physical and mental stamina, then I remove distractions and quiet myself. This might include turning off the TV, lighting a candle and sitting still, meditating on Scripture, or finding a quiet place simply to listen to God. Even with a houseful of busy kids, Mama can declare quiet time. I tend to disguise it as a game of "Let's pretend we're at the library. Everyone get a book and let's snuggle." It may require creativity, but it is possible, at least for a little while.

Baby step: Choose an option from the last paragraph and the next time you feel exhausted, make it your go-to solution.

Fighting Emotional Fatigue

Then there is the tired feeling that often makes us want to throw in the towel—emotional fatigue. The roller-coaster ride of human emotions can be daunting and cruel at times. At the end of the ride, we are worn out and dizzy. The weariness that results from emotional stress is complex and sometimes unpreventable. Perhaps you feel angry and upset because of an unfair circumstance, but once you resolve the problem, you hit a wave of relief. Maybe you are traveling the valley of losing a loved one. You hold grief in one hand when thinking of the anticipated loss and joy in the other hand as you do your best to enjoy each moment together.

When I start feeling like the emotional amusement park rides are spinning out of control, then I look for a way to step off the ride and prevent total emotional exhaustion. I stop to write a list of feelings I'm experiencing, and often the exercise of writing them down provides relief. I text or phone a friend and let her know I am struggling with emotions and ask her to pray for me. I ask a close friend or my husband if he or she would mind listening to my heart. Dealing with emotional fatigue typically requires a pause and recollection.

Baby step: Stop right now to think about the emotions you've experienced in the last few hours or day. If you feel emotionally weary, choose one of the options in the last paragraph and act on it right now.

Fighting Spiritual Fatigue

Spiritually we tire of facing the same temptations and trials. We're weary of trying so hard to understand God's plan for our lives. We might be tired from waiting on a change to take place. While spiritual battles require hand-to-hand combat, we do not fight this war alone. Our strength to take one more step against the Enemy comes from God. As the psalmist declares, "I was pushed hard, so that I was falling, but the LORD helped me" (118:13).

Moving from spiritually exhausted to energetic requires supernatural strength. While we know supernatural strength comes from

God, how can we gather it? Through reading God's Word, spending time in prayer, meeting with other Christians, and sharing our hearts.

When Matt and I received the news of Taylor's terminal diagnosis, we were tempted to stay home from church because the weariness of the battle overwhelmed us. But we knew that one of the best places to be that Sunday morning was at church worshiping with others and listening to our pastor preach God's Word.

Baby step: Determine to meet with other Christians within the next week. Find a community group, Bible study group, or online Christian group.

Why Fatigue Is a Fight

Why does it seem that we Christians are an oh-so-tired people? In an age when so much physical work is streamlined through machinery and mental work is shortened by technology, it would seem that fatigue shouldn't be the same issue it was centuries ago.

When I asked on my Facebook page why we tire easily, our community offered several suggestions for the reasons. Perhaps you can relate to one or more.

- We are constantly on the go . . . never taking time for ourselves. . . . We expect too much out of ourselves, and for some of us, it is because of a health issue.
- We are bombarded by media and/or we allow ourselves to become too involved with social media to the point we are tired from information overload.
- Because we don't take time to stop and rest. We do too much, we don't prioritize correctly, and we're inefficient. We also don't eat properly—fueling our bodies the right way is important.

- Because we glorify busy. Sometimes it feels like I'm told I'm not a "real" mom/wife/daughter if I'm not constantly on the go. Yes, there are tasks, chores, and things that *have* to be done, but when we make the busy into a competition between each other, we're in for trouble.

Do you notice a pattern to these reasons for being too tired? When I thought about my own experiences, I realized it's because of excess. We have so many options vying for our time that we have difficulty maintaining a simple lifestyle. Our choices become overbearing because we choose to do too many things. For instance, social media tires us because we consume too much of what can be a good thing.

Choosing to curb weariness before it grips us is a great choice. But like the children of Israel wandering in the desert, we don't always have a choice in our circumstances. We fight an uphill battle of fatigue with no real rest in sight. Then what? We can take the principles gleaned from the Israelites and Moses and apply them to our lives.

Executing a to-do list should follow establishing a to-be list. God has specifically chosen you for the tasks he has given you. No one else has your same set of skills and talents. The work God has for you can be completed only by you. God chose you for the job, and he will provide the strength you need to do it. Recognizing who God created you to be will enable you to do what he is calling you to do.

Mama's Boxing Gloves

Whenever I would go to the store or post office or anywhere with my mom, people would smile and want to talk to her. She always had a listening ear, and no matter how busy she was with her nine children or housework or church work, she took time for others. Even when she didn't know them well. When she saw a need, she did her best to meet it.

When the church choir leader and his wife moved back to our small town because she had cancer, my mom went to visit her. Between my college semesters, I'd ask my mom why she continually visited this woman she hardly knew. Mom's answer?

"Sometimes we don't fully understand why we are doing things. We just know that God wants us to do them."

What began with one short visit turned into days upon days of visits. No one knew how sick the chemo was going to make this dear woman. No one knew that day after day, she would vomit for hours while my mom held her bedpan and whispered God's love over her. No one knew that her husband would need meals not for a few weeks but for almost two years. No one knew that several days a week for those years, my mom would read Scripture and pray with this extremely ill lady with whom she wasn't even a close friend prior to cancer.

I have no doubt that my mom was exhausted during those two years. She did all the above while still caring for her own family and home. She tried to schedule the visits while we were in school. Then she would pick us up from school and cook and supervise homework. Almost every evening she would take a meal or two to this woman's home and then return to feed her own family. She could have said that her life was too full to keep doing what she had started. I think it would have been okay; everyone involved would have understood. But she would not stop what she knew God wanted her to start. She simply drew strength from the Lord through spending time with him. She guarded this time with him carefully each evening, and this enabled her to fight fatigue in advance of its appearance.

Then eight years later, cancer picked a fight with Mom. The fight was fierce, and the battle was short at less than six months. One of the days just before Mom died, her eyes peered up from the hospital bed at home, and she caught a glimpse of my sister crying. The words somehow made it through her lips and she said, "Everything is going to be all right."

Even in the depths of her own suffering, she wasn't too tired to encourage someone else to keep going. Relying on God for strength had been her habit for so long that she didn't know any other way of living.

What a moment it must have been when Mom crossed over Jordan and met her friend, the choir director's wife, at the pearly gate! While cancer ended their lives on earth, I'd love to hear the alto section of heaven's choir sounding out strong with these two persevering women.

I can't remember my mama ever telling me not to give up when I'm tired. She never had to. She simply lived it. Her example has reminded me time after time that exhaustion is never a reason to give up. From her, I learned that when you feel too tired to keep going, remember that God is never tired. He is our true source of strength, and he is always right there to provide the strength we need to take one more step.

～ ～ ～

Pillars of Truth to Lean On

Whether you find yourself a bit tired or bone weary, these Bible verses will remind you that strength comes from the Lord.

- Awesome is God from his sanctuary; the God of Israel—he is the one who gives power and strength to his people. Blessed be God! (Psalm 68:35)

- You are my hiding place and my shield; I hope in your word. (Psalm 119:114)

- It is in vain that you rise up early and go late to rest, eating the bread of anxious toil; for he gives to his beloved sleep. (Psalm 127:2)

- Have you not known? Have you not heard? The LORD is the everlasting God, the Creator of the ends of the earth. He does not faint or grow weary; his understanding is unsearchable. He gives power to the faint, and to him who has no might he increases strength. Even youths shall faint and be weary, and young men shall fall exhausted; but they who wait for the LORD shall renew their strength; they shall mount up with wings like eagles; they shall run and not be weary; they shall walk and not faint. (Isaiah 40:28–31)

- Come to me, all who labor and are heavy laden, and I will give you rest. Take my yoke upon you, and learn from me, for I am gentle and lowly in heart, and you will find rest for your souls. (Matthew 11:28–29)

Stepping Stone #11

Fighting fatigue requires proactive, rather than reactive, measures. Think about how you want to be remembered and ask yourself if you are being who you believe God wants you to be. Write down five things you want to *be,* such as loving, gracious, honest, unrushed, purposeful, consistent, persistent, etc. When you are rested, you will find it easier to be who you want to be! Choose two or more of the "baby steps" in this chapter and record in your *One More Step* journal four things to do to help you learn how to battle fatigue. Now pray over both lists, asking God to help you intentionally focus on resting well in him.

twelve

Someone to Lean On

*Though sometimes the path seems rough
and steep, see His footprints all the way.*

—Luther B. Bridgers

oneliness can strike at the oddest times and in the oddest places. Have you ever noticed that? At times I've been home alone and have missed the physical presence of my family. (Okay, it's rare, but it has happened!) Just the fact that I was home by myself caused me to feel lonely. Then at other times I've stood in a crowded room and yet felt completely and utterly alone. The physical presence of others had nothing to do with how I felt in that particular environment. A mental, emotional, or spiritual connection was missing.

It's a lonely road when you're the parent of a special-needs child. When we first received Taylor's diagnosis, there was no social media. Online forums were the closest means of finding and communicating with others who had children diagnosed with MPS. The doctor's office staff understood the importance of connecting families with like children, and a few months after we received Taylor's diagnosis, the phone rang.

A secretary from the doctor's office called specifically to let us know that another family who lived an hour away had a daughter with Taylor's type of MPS, also known as Sanfilippo syndrome. They wanted to know if we would like to talk or meet. Would we ever!

From the first day they met, Taylor and Brianna loved each other. Their giggles caused a ripple effect on everyone around them. As our families spent time together, our hearts were knit together and we pondered what it might be like to give more families the opportunity to connect.

So we decided to host a family gathering and invite all the area families we could find. Through doctor's offices, the National MPS Society, and the online forum, we collected addresses and mailed invitations. Three months later, twenty-five people enjoyed the first Ohio MPS Family Gathering as a day of delicious food and companionship. Watching loneliness dissipate from the eyes of parents empowered hearts—both ours and theirs.

Heaven called Brianna home five years later and these same families, along with ours, were stricken with grief. Uniting hearts in beautiful relationship was just one of the many gifts of life Brianna gave. Just a few weeks ago, our family hosted the twelfth annual MPS gathering, where almost two hundred family members and sixteen children affected by MPS attended.

As the Scriptures say, "Two are better than one, because they have a good reward for their toil" (Ecclesiastes 4:9). Two are so much better than one.

Feeling alone in our battles and struggles can often initiate the feeling of wanting to give up. Why?

Wired for Relationship

At the beginning of time, nothing but darkness existed. No world. No sun, moon, and stars. Not even light. Then God spoke. As he spoke the heaven and earth into existence, his spirit moved over the earth. He opened his mouth to tell light to form. Then he reviewed his handiwork and saw that it was good. He commanded the darkness to be separated from the light, thereby creating day and night. His lips whispered the partitions of land and water; he spoke every green thing into being. God flung the sun, moon, and stars into space, and he saw that they were good. The Creator shaped and formed creatures of all kinds, and he filled the oceans and covered the mountains with beautiful inhabitants.

Each day as the entire universe took shape under the Almighty's hand, God paused to exclaim over the goodness. Every single thing that he made was good. What a delightful pause this must have been as the God of glory observed his creation.

On the sixth day, God designed a masterpiece unlike any other. Using his own image and likeness, he sculpted man. After constructing bones and muscles and molding matter and mind into one, he then breathed into his creation. Man became a living soul. God then stepped back to assess his work. The review at the end of the workday indicated this was not just good. God declared this work to be *very good*.

However, after declaring his masterpiece to be very good, God saw a problem. Was there a fur malfunction? Did a plant receive the wrong fruit? Did a particular star shine too brightly? No, for the first time in all of creation, God declared something was not good: "It is not good that the man should be alone; I will make him a helper fit for him" (Genesis 2:18).

Since the beginning of time, God recognized the human need for companionship, fellowship, and camaraderie. He created a solution to the problem of being alone: he created another human being to fill the need. Loneliness is not good; God said so. He wired humans for relationship. God created us with the need for connection to others like us. One of our basic instinctual needs is relationship—mental, emotional, spiritual, and physical.

The response to feelings of loneliness is affected by both personality and background; as a result, individual reactions are different. For instance, my first reaction to sitting at a conference table where I know no one is to read, because that is my comfort zone. I search out any printed conference material and devour it. I check the conference hashtag and retweet my favorite speaker. Slowly adjusting to the environment, I eventually brave myself into smiling at the people at the table and introducing myself to them. But this is a gradual process for me. It's just not part of my personality to "throw myself" at people immediately.

If your personality is more extroverted, then you enjoy meeting new people. Maybe your initial reaction to a conference table of new faces is to immediately walk around and shake hands with each person.

We all have a natural response to loneliness, but regardless, we need to consider if it is the right one.

The right response is to build relationships, and how do we know this? God created relationships to bridge the gap he saw as "not good." The interesting thing is that even if our best friend is dropped right into our lap, we need to respond and then engage in conversation. In order to build relationships, we must be proactive in some manner.

Finding the right spouse requires seeking. Making the right friends requires good decisions. Discovering the church or Bible study group or small group or prayer group God has for us requires trying. The connections we seek may not necessarily exist right in front of us; they may require a willingness to search before we find them. Sometimes seasonal relationships stem from differing circumstances. Life changes and, therefore, friendships change. Regardless of the means, relationship is vital to success in life. The wisest man to live, Solomon, explained the need for relationships like this:

> Two are better than one, because they have a good reward for
> their toil. For if they fall, one will lift up his fellow. But woe to
> him who is alone when he falls and has not another to lift him
> up! Again, if two lie together, they keep warm, but how can one

keep warm alone? And though a man might prevail against one who is alone, two will withstand him—a threefold cord is not quickly broken. (Ecclesiastes 4:9–12)

Defeating Loneliness

I get it. You get it. We all get it. It's not good to continually be alone. If loneliness is the reason you feel like giving up, then beating the odds of loneliness demands that you find strength to take one more step, even a teeny, tiny baby step of some sort. Perhaps the baby step is to make that phone call. Or to reach out on social media. You could send an e-mail. Or maybe even introduce yourself to someone new in a community or church setting.

Have you ever heard a Christian remark that he just doesn't feel connected to a church, but his attendance is weak? Or maybe he is physically present in every possible service, but he continually chooses to limit conversations or interactions with others? Building relationships necessitates not only a baby-step mentality but also consistent effort. While this process can seem overwhelming or exhausting, the rewards are worth the effort. As Solomon stated, we gain someone to help us pick up our weary feet when we can't do it on our own.

When I've limited my conversation with others, sometimes I think, *Well, that's okay. At least I didn't say anything wrong. It's better to say nothing than to say something wrong.* And that's certainly true. And it's biblical: it is better to say nothing than to say something wrong. "When words are many, transgression is not lacking, but whoever restrains his lips is prudent" (Proverbs 10:19). But I'm about to sound out a confession alarm here.

Being proud that I didn't say anything negative is sometimes just an excuse for all the things I wish I could say. Or an excuse for not knowing what to say.

Saying nothing isn't necessarily a signal that my heart is right. Sometimes it's just a sign that I managed to keep my mouth shut. The surface problem is that we need to close our mouths; the spiritual problem is that we need to open our hearts. Opening our hearts will help us overcome the loneliness that constrains us.

Do you know what is far more beautiful than a closely-minded mouth? An open-hearted soul. One who loves and cares and doesn't fear the risk of sharing love and care. We often take better care of our mouths than our souls because the effect of our words on others is visible. All the while, we ignore the heart of the problem, thinking that no one sees it. But someone does see it. The Bible says that "man looks on the outward appearance, but the LORD looks on the heart" (1 Samuel 16:7).

A kind, open heart is far more beautiful than a harsh, closed mouth. The cure for loneliness is opening our hearts. In order to ditch feelings of loneliness, our hearts must be receptive to those God places in front of us. This isn't an easy step because we all carry baggage from previous relationships. Sometimes that baggage is so heavy that we can't pack it around. Instead of letting it go, we use it to build a barricade and prevent any relationships, even the healthy ones God wants us to enjoy. By preventing healthy relationships, we further establish our own loneliness.

Maybe you're like me and you just don't know what to say to others. The dark cloud of silence and awkwardness looms before you, and opening your heart to others is just plain scary. When I feel afraid to open myself to others, I remember this: "It is the LORD who goes before you. He will be with you; he will not leave you or forsake you. Do not fear or be dismayed" (Deuteronomy 31:8).

We can rely on him to fill our mouths with the words that he would have us say. Not only is he with us, but he goes before us, preparing the way. With him going before us, we need not be afraid of losing the words to say or being mistakenly judged by another. The beauty of his nearness allows us to ask him freely to give us our words.

Maybe you are afraid others won't understand your situation. That they might view you as a complainer or whiner or think something of you that is not true. Perhaps someone has been mean to you, even without purposely intending to be. While there are all sorts of reasons that we fear opening ourselves to others, opening an authentic heart will promote community. Sharing ourselves with others through conversation and daily living builds relationships, making the sweet sweeter and the bitter easier to swallow.

Making the choice to consistently extend ourselves to new relationships will increase relational bonds and decrease loneliness. I've found it easier to make the choice to be open to new friendships or deepen friendships when I set minigoals. Here are a few ideas for mini relationship goals:

- This week I'm going to text or call two friends with whom I'm already connected, just to check on them.
- At church on Sunday, I'm going to meet one new person in my small group, Sunday school class, or the worship service and follow up by connecting on social media or requesting her e-mail address or phone number.
- This month I want to have at least one coffee date with a close friend, so I need to schedule it this week.
- This month I want to write notes to three other women in a busy season of life to encourage their hearts. (I think that could be any woman!)

I've found that when I set friendship goals of a smaller nature and make the time to follow through on those goals, I can look back and see the progress I've made in combating loneliness. By reaching out to others, I find myself centered on their needs and less focused on my own. As a result, I feel less lonely and more connected.

Many times loneliness sets in due to circumstances that limit your availability. Maybe you work a night shift or evening shift and your schedule doesn't correlate with most of your friends' or family's schedules. Perhaps your situation includes working part-time while raising a family of three kids under five years of age. Such confining schedules can make it challenging to find time to connect with family, friends, or neighbors.

Whatever the reason, combating loneliness during these seasons can require creativity. In lieu of a face-to-face meeting, you could schedule a video chat. Maybe this is a time to find an Internet community group with those of similar interests or needs. If participating in a community or church Bible study is a challenge due to scheduling, you could find an online Bible study in which to participate. Purposeful online connections can bridge the gap in schedules, but real-life, face-to-face community will revive your spirit like nothing else. The point is that connecting with others requires reaching out, and sometimes this will include thinking outside the box.

The Two Most Powerful Words

Recently two e-mails appeared in my inbox at once. Both were from moms of special-needs children who were experiencing hardships. Each is on a pilgrimage to find a diagnosis and pursue treatment for a child. Such a long, hard journey.

In responding to their e-mails, I came to a realization—one that includes a two-word combo that packs more power than any two words in the English language.

The combo comes into play when an individual needs prayer and someone else comes along to pray. Another person joins in and before you know it, a whole prayer band has formed to ask God to work in precious lives. Or when someone admits to needing help in a certain area and a friend says, "Oh, I need help in that area also." Maybe the pastor began his sermon with his own dilemma, and after hearing his story, your heart agreed with his on the topic. Or you read an article, and afterward you felt led to share it on social media because the tug on your heart was so strong you couldn't help yourself.

You see, all of these examples reveal what I believe to be perhaps the most empowering two-word team. They are the two simple words of *me too*.

Can you imagine what would happen if our hearts were open for opportunities to empower others with this tiny duo?

"I'm tired."
"Me too. Want to get some coffee?"

"I need someone to help me stay accountable to read God's Word each day."
"Me too. Let's check in with each other once a week."

"I want to spend more time in prayer."
"Me too. Want to pray together or text each other every Monday morning?"

I've found that once a conversation is started, we discover common interests and goals. Pretty soon, we've discovered a few books we both love or a hobby we wish we had time for. As C. S. Lewis states, "Friendship . . . is born at the moment when one man says to another 'What! You too? I thought that no one but myself . . .'"[5]

With two words of simple vocabulary, a person can be transported from an island of loneliness to a continent of cure. The comfort of another human being simply agreeing to our life dilemmas is powerful indeed.

The Gift of His Presence

Even more powerful is the thought of how much Jesus suffered to give us this affirmation. Jesus loves us so much that he gave himself for us. He died on the cross and rose again that we could have eternal life. The Son of God determined to live within the confines of a human body and experienced earthly life in the form of human development and limitations. He suffered pain and hunger and betrayal and hurt. He endured heartache and grief and despair. And loneliness.

All so that he could say two little words to you and me: *me too.*

Jesus promises never to leave you. "I will never leave you nor forsake you" (Hebrews 13:5). He promises always to be with you. He loves you beyond what you can fathom. If you feel that you have no one else in the world, Jesus is forever someone to lean on.

～ ～ ～

Pillars of Truth to Lean On

Use these verses to combat loneliness and encourage
yourself to reach out to the world.

- Be strong and courageous. Do not fear or be in dread of
  them, for it is the LORD your God who goes with you. He
  will not leave you or forsake you. (Deuteronomy 31:6)
- God places the lonely in families; he sets the prisoners
  free and gives them joy. (Psalm 68:6, NLT)
- I am continually with you; you hold my right hand.
  (Psalm 73:23)
- O LORD, you have searched me and known me! You
  know when I sit down and when I rise up; you discern
  my thoughts from afar. You search out my path and
  my lying down and are acquainted with all my ways.
  (Psalm 139:1–3)

Stepping Stone #12

Defeating loneliness requires being willing to risk reaching out to Jesus and to others. Using the ideas in this chapter, write down one minigoal to help you foster intentional relationships with other Christians, and keep yourself accountable to follow through within the week. Then write down your loneliness number on a scale of 1–10, with 1 being least lonely and 10 the loneliest. At the end of the week, write down your number again, as well as three reasons you feel your minigoal was successful or unsuccessful. Write a prayer of thanks in your *One More Step* journal declaring that Jesus is always with you and will never leave you. Praise him for being your "someone to lean on"!

thirteen

Your Signature Here

Take my will, and make it Thine; it shall be
no longer mine.

—Frances R. Havergal

I stepped out of the van, and the sun beamed down on my legs. A quick glance at the phone revealed I didn't have much time. The combination of heat and caring for my family was taking a toll, and I breathed a prayer before going into the grocery store.

Lord, I know it might seem crazy to pray over grocery shopping, but please help me get through this trip. Don't let me buy anything I shouldn't and keep me focused to finish on time. It would be great if I didn't have to return this week.

With coupons and list in hand, I psyched myself up for a personal version of *Grocery Games*. I had one hour and no children with me. This should seem like a vacation, right? If I could make it through the store and get everything on the list before the hour was up, I decided I would treat myself. And the treat? A can of root beer from the outdoor pop machine. Not just any root beer. A cold and frothy A&W.

I executed the plan precisely and raided each aisle expertly. Like a marathon runner focused on the finish, mile twenty-six under my belt, I flew out of the grocery store doors the same way I entered, thanking the Lord it was over.

I could hardly wait to take the first sip of that icy cold root beer. I slipped the fifty cents into the machine (don't even try to guess my age) and heard the clink, clank, *clunk*. Preparing to enjoy my long-awaited prize, I peered into the machine opening. But I didn't see an icy cold can of root beer.

Instead, a bird plopped out on the concrete and hopped around in a dazed and confused state.

I felt a set of eyes staring at me and looked up to see a store employee who had been moving carts. He shook his head and said, "Did you see that? No one will ever believe this."

I had to think he was right. Such a strange experience, this wild exchange of expectations.

I had prayed, I had followed through on the work, and when I stood at the machine, fully anticipating my root beer, what happened?

No root beer. I got a bird. Apparently the bird had snuggled up in the machine for a warm sleeping place. When my root beer plunked down through the machine, it hit him on the head, soundly knocking him back out to civilization. While he reveled in the glory of sunlight, I reveled in the mystery of receiving a bird from a pop machine.

Sounds like life to me.

You put your time in at work, fully expecting a raise when you were called into the boss's office, but instead you were issued a layoff notice. Or your struggle with infertility finally yielded a viable pregnancy, only to miscarry the baby at seventeen weeks. Maybe the man you married seems to have changed dramatically, and now you don't know each other anymore. Perhaps the tumor the doctor believed to be benign was cancerous after all.

Sometimes we're standing at the machine of life, eagerly anticipating our root beer, only to get something completely and totally different . . . a bird.

Gideon's Choice

The Midianites oppressed Gideon's people, the children of Israel, for seven years after God judged them for continually doing evil. The Israelites had resorted to living in caves and rock crevices to stay safe. Every crop they planted was stolen.

As we enter the story in Judges 6, Gideon had creatively attempted to provide food for his family. He didn't need Pinterest to tell him that the most ideal place to thresh wheat was not in the winepress. While the environment was not the best location for the job, Gideon chose it so he wouldn't be seen and the food stolen. In the midst of Gideon's work, an angel appeared to him.

The angel's introductory words? "The LORD is with you, O mighty man of valor" (verse 12).

Can you imagine how Gideon felt in that moment? He was hiding from the Midianites, his family was oppressed and living in caves, yet the angel said, "The LORD is with you." While I feel sure that the angel's words were intended to encourage, perhaps even honor, I think my response might have been the same as Gideon's: "If the LORD is with us, why then has all this happened to us? And where are all his wonderful deeds that our fathers recounted to us, saying, 'Did not the LORD bring us up from Egypt?' But now the LORD has forsaken us and given us into the hand of Midian" (verse 13).

We get a peek into Gideon's humanity. While the angel called Gideon his warrior, Gideon's response was, "Oh really? I have no idea what you're talking about. I didn't sign up for this."

I wish we could visually see Gideon's body as he was threshing the wheat. I wonder if his shoulders slumped. Did he drag his feet with each step? Was the negative internal chatter about to burst out of his head? Was he tired of trying? Was he flat out exhausted?

We do know his circumstances were far less than ideal and he didn't see any sign of change. Instead, he wanted to know what happened to God's miracles his forefathers personally observed. Perhaps he thought, *Why do they get to hit the easy button, and meanwhile, I'm hiding out in grape world trying to thresh wheat—a job that isn't meant to be performed in this environment? Where is my miracle?*

I've felt that way. Have you? I've thought everyone else in my neighborhood seemed to be doing okay, but why was I having such a hard time? My family seemed to have it all together, so why couldn't I encounter the same success? I never asked for this difficult circumstance. This issue was completely unexpected. I didn't sign up for this job. Where is *my* miracle?

Yet the angel responded to Gideon: "Go in this might of yours and save Israel from the hand of Midian; do not I send you?" (verse 14).

God asked Gideon a personal question: "Am I not the one sending you?"

I believe God was reiterating to Gideon: *You know me, Gideon. We have a relationship and you know who I am—the God of the universe.* While Gideon questioned God boldly over his people's suffering, he had no desire to hit the battlefield. Essentially he said, "What am I supposed to do? My tribe is the least in Israel, my family is the lowest in my tribe, and I am the youngest in my father's house. You surely have the wrong guy."

And again God responded: "But I will be with you, and you shall strike the Midianites as one man" (verse 16).

God's response was, "I'm going to be with you."

Still, Gideon struggled with trusting God. So he requested a sign that God truly was with him and he wasn't just dreaming the whole scenario. God lovingly provided Gideon with the affirmation he sought. Long story short, Gideon followed God's instructions and God delivered the Israelites from the Midianites.

While the battle ended in victory, it wasn't one that Gideon wanted to begin. He didn't choose his circumstances; they were beyond his control. He didn't like the resolution; after all, he really didn't want to be a part. He came up with every excuse not to go to war, but his excuses were invalid. His background didn't matter and his heritage was not an issue. His skill set was precisely what God desired for the situation. God had handpicked Gideon specifically for the job. And the best part? Gideon wasn't going alone. God would be with him every step. God could see Gideon on the other side of victory all along.

Gideon felt as I did at the beginning of this chapter. He was standing at the pop machine of life, waiting for his root beer, when instead a bird dropped at his feet. He was waiting for God to miraculously deliver his people, and instead something completely unforeseen happened. When the angel unexpectedly came to him, Gideon had a choice to make. He could choose to accept the unexpected or turn away in anger.

What do you do when your focus is fixed on a certain outcome, but the unexpected happens? That time you worked on the project with more dedication than ever, but it didn't make the cut. Your boss chose to highlight someone else's work and put him forward for promotion. Or maybe it was the six-month period when you followed the doctor's orders to the last detail, but the cancer returned anyway. Perhaps your long-awaited pregnancy finally became a reality and you found your arms filled with a beautiful baby, but your beautiful baby was born with Down syndrome. Maybe you finally reached retirement and desperately need a slower change of pace, but suddenly a young child in the extended family needed

care and you were it. Was it your parent who was diagnosed with the beginning stages of Alzheimer's? Your teenage daughter encountering severe depression?

I don't have to continue giving examples, because you've been there,
probably more than once. You didn't sign up for this _____
(fill in the blank), and now what?

No one really wants to edit the project and present it to the boss a
fourth, fifth, or sixth time. No one wants to fight cancer again. No one
dreams of having anything other than a perfectly healthy baby. No one
projects her retirement years will be spent caring daily for a young child
with great needs. No one wants to research how to make her home safe
for someone losing his memory. No one wants to try to understand depression symptoms or arrange for doctors or medication or counseling for
her teen.

You face the same choice that Gideon faced when the angel spoke to
him: accept the unanticipated assignment and move forward, or continue
the restricted routine and miss the opportunity.

So how did Gideon do it? How did he make the transition from "No
way" to "I'm all in"? How did he get from the point of wanting to run
away to the point of following through with God's plan? Let's dissect his
journey of discovering faith to keep trying.

Gideon's Discovery

Gideon's story outlines each step to his personal discovery of strength to
keep going, even when he felt like giving up. While we initially meet him
in the pit of despair where he had lingered for some time, he didn't stay
there.

Gideon wished to live in a previous miracle-working era and see all
that his ancestors had seen, but all the wishing in the world wouldn't

change his incredibly desperate circumstances. His first step out of the pit? Instead of wishing for the miracles of his forefathers, he accepted his assignment. It was time for Gideon to get up and move. At the point of realizing the truth of his situation, that God was indeed calling him to a greater purpose, he needed to stop wishing and start working. **Working toward a milestone will always accomplish more than wishing for a miracle.**

Gideon had the opportunity to be part of the miracle, rather than simply watch the miracle. Is there any greater honor? I believe that God is still in the miracle-working business, but many times we only want to see the miracle and not be a part of the miracle-working solution.

Gideon realized the time to change was the present. While he wasn't completely sure what the future would look like, his excuses weren't valid and he recognized this. It was time to stop dwelling on all the reasons he wasn't equipped to fight the battle.

A collection of excuses for why we can't do something will never evolve into a treasury of reasons we did.

But how could he stop looking at his own weaknesses? By shifting his focus and looking toward the true Source of strength. He realized who was calling him to fight—God almighty, the Lord of hosts. The call to battle wasn't for Gideon to go it alone; it was for him to fight in the strength of the Lord.

What to Do When God Meets You

I love what Gideon did once he recognized that his strength for the battle would be all on God—he built an altar. In the Old Testament, altars were built as memorials for the places God met someone. Gideon respected the experience of meeting God, and he reacted in honor and sacrifice. He didn't wait for a better time or a better place. He built an altar right where he was, the exact place where God met him.

When you are deep in that desperate space and God meets you, don't walk away and forget it before the week is over. Just like Gideon, embrace the opportunity to remember where God met you. **Make a memorial when God meets you miraculously.**

Though your neighbors might have a few things to say if you slaughtered an animal and built an altar in your backyard, you can still purposefully make a memory of God confirming his strength in you. How? If you're reading Scripture and the words leap from the page into your heart, then write them in a Scripture journal. Or highlight them so that each time you read them in the future, you will remember how you felt when God spoke to your heart. If you're listening to a sermon, write a few of the statements that stick with you and date them. Keep them in a special binder where you can review them from time to time. If you're an artist, paint a picture. Give yourself an image to remember what it was like when God met with you. If you're out in nature, pick up a small stone and put it in your pocket. Take it home and place it on the kitchen windowsill or in a collection jar; add a little slip of paper with a verse or word that you knew God impressed on your heart. If the worship service brought you to a place of strength, then put those songs on your smartphone so you can listen to them time and time again. If you're a musician, write a song and sing it. If you're a poet, carve out the words and share them. No matter the means, make a memorial of the moment you realized that God is your strength and the battle belongs to him.

Making a memorial also serves as battle preparation. When you're in the middle of the fight and you need refreshment, pausing to look back at the memory of where God met you in his strength is going to fuel you forward.

When God first impressed on my heart to teach Bible studies, I felt kind of foolish and completely unqualified. How did I know that God was speaking to me? Could this be a dream? Could I have made this up? One night as I studied and read in my bed, I wept with nervous joy because I knew without a doubt that God's presence met with me. This is my journal entry:

1-5-09

I believe that God wants me to teach his Word and he will provide a way to do so. I believe that God wants the Bible study on Hannah to be continued beyond writing it down. I believe that God is going to do a beyond-my-asking-or-thinking thing in my life.

You see, I didn't have the how, when, where, or with whom answers. I somehow knew that I needed to write it down, and I had to find a way to remember this moment for the future. I can't tell you how many times I've gone back to this journal I keep tucked in the nightstand drawer. It helps me remember that God still meets with his people today. In unexpected places and unanticipated ways. My heart beats with the words often attributed to Elisabeth Elliot: "We never know what God has up His sleeve. You never know what might happen; you only know what you have to do now."

The Dotted Line

Many years ago, for several months, I wrestled with what I believed God was whispering to my heart. I felt that he told me, *Serve me wholeheartedly. Tell others of me. Just give me what you have—brokenness and all.*

Share your community Bible study online. I want you to inspire women to grow their faith and live it out daily.

But, Lord, I responded, *you know I'm just an everyday person. I mostly stay at home with lots of little ones and a special-needs child. I can barely get to the grocery store, much less serve in the community. It's a struggle. We have no family living close by, and I don't have much help. I'm not an outgoing person. I don't have much money; we live by faith. And I don't have any professional training to write or speak. I have no idea how all this could work.*

He answered, *Trust me.*

But no one will believe me. They'll think I'm crazy. And they'll ignore me.

Do you love me? he replied.

More than anything. But I still struggled until finally I responded, *Okay. I'll do whatever you want. You can have all of me—the cracks, the pieces, the fragments. The divorce, my mom's death, my daughter's terminal illness, the negative emotions, and the blessings of today. I give it all to you. Even the leftovers. But if you want me to tell others about you, then you're going to have to bring the people to me. You're going to have to tell me what to say. And you're going to have to show me what to do.*

If God had given me an actual piece of paper, I would have scribbled my name on the dotted line.

With loving patience, he affirmed my heart. *Girl, just wait and see what I'm going to do.*

Spring turned into summer, and how time flies when you care for a houseful of children. I didn't really notice anything different throughout the next few months. But one particular day, I noticed an extra busyness centered at the front door of my home. The UPS man. Neighbor children. Piano students and their parents.

Twenty-seven people visited our house that day.

And toward the end of the day God whispered, *I brought them to you.*

In awe, the tears flowed as I humbly replied, *Wow. Yes, you did.*

And I glanced back at the signature line, the day I said yes to God's assignment.

I had asked God to bring the people to me. Twenty-seven people. I thought that was a lot! But God has quite the sense of humor. Today, six years later, God brings thousands and thousands of people each day to my virtual space at RachelWojo.com.

God's not finished with the project, by any means. My brokenness, transformed into his beautiful masterpiece, is still an unfinished product, yet it continues to reflect a little more of his light each day through writing and serving my family.

You see, I discovered that he walks with us, infusing his strength into our steps, one by one. I don't have to have a perfect track record or all the answers for the future.

He beckons you too. The assignment? I don't know the details, but it's something you may not necessarily have wanted. A role that wasn't part of your childhood dreams. A task that you don't want to do. An assignment for which you have been chosen and now the Lord is whispering to your heart to sign the dotted line. He affirms your heart with words similar to these: *I know you wanted a root beer. But I have something so much better than that.*

Say yes. Someday you'll look back on the unexpected and think, *I wouldn't have it any other way.*

~ ~ ~

Pillars of Truth to Lean On

When you get something you didn't sign up for, remember
these truths for guidance.

- The steps of a man are established by the LORD,
  when he delights in his way; though he fall, he shall
  not be cast headlong, for the LORD upholds his hand.
  (Psalm 37:23–24)

- God is our refuge and strength, a very present help
  in trouble. Therefore we will not fear though the
  earth gives way, though the mountains be moved
  into the heart of the sea, though its waters roar and
  foam, though the mountains tremble at its swelling.
  (Psalm 46:1–3)

- I will remember the deeds of the LORD; yes, I will
  remember your wonders of old. . . . You are the God
  who works wonders; you have made known your
  might among the peoples. (Psalm 77:11, 14)

- I consider that the sufferings of this present time
  are not worth comparing with the glory that is to
  be revealed to us. (Romans 8:18)

Signing the dotted line of the contract you "didn't sign up for" brings incredible fulfillment and strength from God. Pour your heart out to God regarding the work he has for you to do, whether you know what it is or are still waiting to understand more details.

Write a prayer expressing your thoughts on his purpose and work for your life. Complete the following fill-in-the-blank statement on your own piece of paper or using your *One More Step* journal:

"Today I agree to the position of _____, given to me by God with his supreme knowledge that I am capable because he is my strength. He sees me on the other side of _____ in victory."

Sign this statement as a covenant promise. (And if you're like me, you might need to add a period at the end of your name as an emphasized reminder to your stubborn self.)

fourteen

Sitting on "E"

Little is much when God is in it!

—Kittie L. Suffield

Matt and I experienced God's blessing several times through the gift of children. Our sweet children numbered five altogether after five years of marriage, and graciously, I found myself pregnant once more. (I know! How does this keep happening?) Our happy hearts revealed themselves on our faces, and just a few days shy of the ten-week pregnancy mark, we shared the baby news with our children. The excitement gleamed in their eyes. I could tell they figured that if it made Mom and Dad happy, then it must be a good thing, right?

However, that very night something in my body began to feel "not right," and by the next morning I experienced cramping . . . that turned into bleeding . . . that turned into contractions. Our little baby was not forming properly, and we were never given the privilege to see his or her cherished face. Heartache ravaged my body alongside the pain, and I can't remember ever feeling so helpless and empty. The place in our hearts for a beloved baby sat vacant and barren. Like a blanket covering my spirit, the sorrow covered me entirely. I grieved for the little life we had anticipated joining our family, and I grieved for my children, who cried for the sibling they would never know.

Anticipating what God was going to do through our emptiness was beyond my scope of grief. I scraped myself together enough to continue going through the motions of another day, but looking beyond the next few moments required more than I could muster.

That's how the widow felt in 2 Kings 4. This woman found herself in a state of emptiness on many levels. Her husband had been a just man, serving God and his family. The Bible doesn't tell us exactly what happened to him, just that he was dead.

Existing sparingly until she had virtually nothing left, the widow was driven to request help from the prophet Elisha. If she didn't pay her bills, the loan collectors would take her sons to work off the debt. Her drive to prevent her family from starving and to keep her two sons from becoming slaves spurred the widow to action. Ready to give up completely, yet clutching tightly to the lives of her two sons, she begged Elisha for a miracle to save her family.

After she approached the prophet with her problem, he asked her, "What do you have?"

Can you imagine her facial expression? Emptiness had overtaken her household and she had nothing left. Nothing. No money, no heritage, not a scrap. On top of this, her heart held empty places of longing for her husband. I mean, if she had something to work with, why would she stand before the prophet asking for help? She took a deep breath and replied to him that she had nothing except one jar of oil.

But what could a tiny bottle of oil do? I mean, really, without flour, the oil was useless. And it was such a small amount. One jar. What could she possibly do with one jar of oil?

However, Elisha gave the widow specific instructions for that oil. He told the widow to borrow from her neighbors every bottle and jar she could find. The more, the merrier. He wanted her to have her sons help. When she couldn't borrow any more, he told her to close all the windows and doors of her house and start pouring oil from her one small bottle into all the borrowed jars. When one bottle was filled, she was to set it aside and fill the next.

With all the faith she could muster, at her point of giving up, the widow followed Elisha's instructions to the letter. She borrowed every vessel she could. Once she had borrowed the jars, she and her sons shut up the house, every nook and cranny. By faith, she began the pouring process. Her tiny bottle of oil held barely enough to make one loaf of bread if she'd had the flour to do so. Maybe she felt foolish in the logic of the circumstances, yet desperation propelled her forward. Then God stepped in and the oil continued to flow. What she lacked in tangibility, she filled with faith, while the almighty God provided. By God's power, every borrowed jar and bottle was filled to the brim with oil.

Emptiness of Soul

Emptiness is a difficult emotion to describe. It is that feeling you have not just when you are tired but when you have given everything you've got. Nothing remains, whether you've exhausted your resources or they were snatched from you. When you feel empty, it's as though a piece of your soul is missing. Maybe you are grieving the loss of a loved one and the grief is causing you to feel empty. Perhaps your heart aches with the space left by one you love who didn't return your love. Sometimes the emptiness comes from feeling unfulfilled in your goals or dreams. Life can be so full, yet without a deep-heart satisfaction, you continually wrestle to grab hold of complete contentment.

When you feel that you have nothing left but a vacant spirit, the challenge is obvious. This is where the widow found herself when she approached Elisha. Can you imagine the thoughts raiding the widow's mind? *I don't know what Elisha is thinking. I hate borrowing things from others. We're in enough debt already. What good is this one tiny bottle?* And in the pit of her soul, the worst thought lingered: *Unless a miracle takes place, we're going to lose the one thing we do have—one another.*

The challenge in the midst of our emptiness is to see that God fills the gaps. **God invites us to look beyond the little we have to the largeness of what he offers.**

But what it must have been like to start pouring all that oil from one little bottle! I can't imagine the anticipation building in the hearts and minds of the widow and her sons. I have to believe it was all she could do not to tremble. Maybe her hands were visibly shaking. Maybe she choked back a hopeless sob. Once the oil began to flow, I doubt if the woman had a single thought of stopping before she filled all the jars. Her face beamed with joy as she continued to pour, carefully filling every last vessel. The prophet had challenged her hopeless, empty state. He encouraged her to trust that God would fill the empty places of her life.

After she reported her obedience, the prophet further instructed the widow to sell the oil, pay her debts, and live off the profits. The widow happily went home and lived securely. Can you imagine the joy in her heart as she hugged her sons?

The emptiness of the widow is easy to recognize in this story. In fact, I think most of us easily recognize emptiness. We know that something is missing; it's innate. We feel as though we have been searching for fulfillment our entire lives, always seeking satisfaction and contentment, yet never seeming to find it.

The problem is not that we can't see our own emptiness. The problem is that we are lost and confused on how to fill empty soul space. We read more self-help books. We Google more symptoms. We demand more of ourselves. We fill our houses with more stuff and our schedules with more activities. And still something is missing. If only we could get more money . . . more time . . . more family . . . more friends . . . more food . . . more, more, more.

All the while our souls feel empty. Because what we really crave is more of God.

Emptiness of soul can be replaced only by the fullness of God.

The Message paraphrase of Colossians 2:9–10 succinctly describes the human plight of emptiness:

> Everything of God gets expressed in him, so you can see and hear him clearly. You don't need a telescope, a microscope, or a horoscope to realize the fullness of Christ, and the emptiness of the universe without him. When you come to him, that fullness comes together for you, too. His power extends over everything.

God's power extends over everything in this world. Even a little bottle of oil that held only a few ounces could produce beyond its capacity. Even an empty widow with a vacant soul could encounter the fullness of God when she came to him with virtually nothing. When our resources are depleted and we feel empty, no matter the reason, we can be filled when we go to God. Psalm 31:24 provides further instruction on what to do with the problem of emptiness: "Be brave. Be strong. Don't give up. Expect GOD to get here soon" (MSG).

These are the same four points the widow followed. She was brave enough to approach the prophet in her sorrows. She was strong enough to search out and borrow her neighbors' oil bottles. She didn't give up, though all the odds were stacked against her. She acted in faith, anticipating and expecting that God would deliver her.

You see, God was already there. It wasn't as if he didn't know what was going on in her life. It wasn't as if he was busy with other people and couldn't take the time to catch up with her empty pantry or hollow soul. He was about to provide for her in a way beyond her comprehension. What if she had estimated by the weight of the bottle that there was nothing left and she didn't bother to keep trying? What if she had stopped pouring before all the vessels were filled? She would have missed God's best for her, which was to fill *all* the jars. Upon selling them, she would experience fulfillment for the remainder of her life.

He's there for you too. He knows every detail of your life circumstances. He's never too busy, and more than anyone, he understands the craving of your soul for more, because he placed it there. Not only is he there for you, but he knows your current situation and every last detail of your future. His plan includes walking with you every step of the way.

When our needs match those of the widow's, God's promises tell us that he is good (see Psalm 116:5), he works all things for our good (see Romans 8:28), and his work is going to be more than we can dream of (see Ephesians 3:20–21).

His promises are what we must know and claim when we've spent every ounce of strength and sit on empty. We must believe that God is going to work according to his Word. **When we are familiar with God's promises, we can expectantly appreciate the future.**

Yes, it requires bravery. We'll definitely have to rely on his strength. And giving up won't be an option, even if the most microscopic step is all we can muster. Just like the widow, we have to choose to look beyond the little we have left to the largeness of God's presence. Even if we have to pour the oil with a trembling hand, that's better than choosing not to pick up the little oil jar we have.

Filling Heart Vacancies

In the deep fog of grief and total emptiness of soul, I didn't know how to be brave when our baby blessing didn't live to see this world. I couldn't find strength for an hour, much less an entire day. My focus narrowed to the next moment.

Sometimes the boldest thing we can do is just take the next breath.

Have you ever played the child's game of Mother May I? The players stand at one end of the play area, and the leader, who plays the mother, stands at the other end with her back toward the players. The object of the game is to be the first player to reach the mother by requesting to take steps toward her. I felt as if I was playing life's rendition of Mother May I. Only I didn't care about winning. I wasn't sure what to do. I just needed to get in the game. So I took a few teeny, tiny steps. I prayed. I got out of bed each morning and hugged my children. I cried and prayed with my husband. Some baby steps. I soaked up my extended family's encouraging words over the phone. I started to handle routine household tasks and made family meals.

A few of my steps went sideways and didn't seem like steps at all. I tried to attend a monthly church group for mothers but didn't feel comfortable. I made only one meeting that year. Some of the steps were scissor steps and my feet crossed each other, making zero forward progress. I would make it through the day and then when the children were in bed and Matt left for the night shift, I'd find myself unable to hold back the tears. A few times I fell asleep weeping.

But no matter what the steps looked like, I moved one foot after the other. Just one more step; that's all I had to take. After some time, I was able to open my eyes wide enough to anticipate what God wanted to do. I can now see that a part of his plan was to enable me to encourage other families who pass through the journey of miscarriage.

You see, the vacancies God places in our lives are reminders that we live in a temporary world. He uses these spaces to point out that only his power can fill the emptiness. Miraculously, he fills the empty space and reminds us that we need him more than anything. The old vacancy sign in our hearts serves as a beautiful connection to another empty heart of a person who needs to know her vacancy can be filled only by Jesus. The process begins by going to him, then being filled by him, and, finally, relying on his fullness each and every step.

Once we are filled, we have the opportunity to share from the overflow. This sharing often yields beautiful results: connecting people to Christ. When more people get to know Jesus, then God receives the glory.

"As God's grace reaches more and more people, there will be great thanksgiving, and God will receive more and more glory. *That is why we never give up.* Though our bodies are dying, our spirits are being renewed every day" (2 Corinthians 4:15–16, NLT).

This is the more we are searching for.

~ ~ ~

Pillars of Truth to Lean On

When you feel empty and ready to give up, use these verses to fill up instead.

- Our mouth was filled with laughter, and our tongue with shouts of joy; then they said among the nations, "The LORD has done great things for them." (Psalm 126:2)
- May the God of hope fill you with all joy and peace in believing, so that by the power of the Holy Spirit you may abound in hope. (Romans 15:13)
- For the sake of Christ, then, I am content with weaknesses, insults, hardships, persecutions, and calamities. For when I am weak, then I am strong. (2 Corinthians 12:10)
- Though you have not seen him, you love him. Though you do not now see him, you believe in him and rejoice with joy that is inexpressible and filled with glory. (1 Peter 1:8)

Stepping Stone #14

Emptiness of soul can be filled only through the fullness of God. Create a list of your barren heart spaces—the ones with vacancy signs on the door, such as disease, divorce, miscarriage, abortion, addiction, and so on. Now write down the substitutes with which you've attempted to fill the vacancy, such as work, money, success, and so on. Next, pray over these lists and ask God to fill these shallow places to the brim with his love. Write down this prayer in your *One More Step* journal and believe God will use the emptiness to create a connection for revealing his changing power!

fifteen

The Good White Flag

Love so amazing, so divine, demands my soul,
my life, my all.

—Isaac Watts

When the doctors assign a life expectancy number to your child, fear engulfs your soul. Our instinctive reaction to fear is known as the "fight or flight" mechanism. Upon diagnosis, mine kicked in full force. While overwhelming occasions caused flareups of "flight," my instinct leaned more toward "fight." So fight we did.

I knew that when Taylor lost a skill, she would not regain it, due to neurological degeneration. Her inability to ever put her own socks on again was evidence of this fact. My list-making habit kicked in, and I verbally ensured that all school personnel understood why routines were necessary and important, probably too often for their liking. Taylor's education team and I established regular schedules for speech, occupational, and physical therapies, and through her daily routine, Taylor practiced every skill she possessed. During interventional education planning meetings and home healthcare meetings, I emphasized things like why Taylor should continue to hold and drink from a sippy cup, why she needed to step into a pull-up style undergarment instead of lying down to be changed, and why she needed to eat in a consistent manner. I reiterated the small details of life day after day in order to maintain her abilities.

Taylor began to lose more stamina and control of her limbs, and this forced us to rethink everything we did, both for her and as a family. She couldn't walk for more than ten paces without assistance, and her pediatrician advised Matt and me to apply for a disabled parking permit. I remember the day I stood in the state Bureau of Motor Vehicles staring at the permit's expiration date. It was five years into the future. I couldn't help but wonder if she would live to need another permit. She could no longer care for herself in any manner, and her brain had deteriorated to the point of having seizures.

As regularly as we practiced daily habits to prevent loss of skill, Taylor's abilities continued to dwindle. Today at age eighteen, three years past the typical life expectancy, we can still coax smiles with chocolate pudding. I'm so glad that Taylor can enjoy a few M&M'S now and then. She manages to walk with assistance, though it is growing more and more difficult.

Last fall as I helped her try to move up the school bus steps, she landed one foot solid and then dangled the next one in the air. I could see her attempt to figure out what she was supposed to do, but the connections in her brain refused to fire properly. Gently I lifted the dangling foot to the next step up.

Her wonderful longtime bus driver, our friend, commented, "She just doesn't know what to do anymore, does she?"

"No," I replied, "but we're trying to fight it as long as we can."

Mentally I checked off the list: *Made it to the bus one more day.*

MPS is hard. The gradual loss of Taylor's skills sometimes makes me cry. It's been more than twelve years since Taylor called me Mommy or sang the Happy Birthday song. I should have recorded her singing more often than I did. In a singsong tone, Taylor would call "Mommmmyyyy?" over and over. I wish I could say I never grew annoyed by her constant requests. Now I crave her echoing voice.

I know that your story is difficult too. Our experiences serve as relational connections. But there's something I've learned that makes life even more difficult. For many of us, rather than embrace life as it is, we look back on the past with regrets. I'm tempted to do so over Taylor's loss of voice. Learning from previous experiences is wise and wonderful. However, we have a tendency to want to change what has happened, especially our mistakes. That desire is not necessarily wrong, but the fact remains that we can't change history. **We can't allow the desire to change the past freeze our ability to move in the present.**

When we allow ourselves to drag the mistakes we've made around with us, we are weighed down and are unable to take the steps God has for us in the present. At some point, we have to surrender yesterday in order to have the necessary strength to take action today. When we begin to see that God has a beautiful future planned, we can let go of days gone by. As C. S. Lewis said, "There are better things ahead than any we leave behind."[6]

Murder, He Wrote

If ever there was a man who had to let go of the past, Moses was the man. In Exodus 2, he was the baby in the bulrushes, hidden by his mother for protection. The king had ordered all baby boys to be thrown in the river. The princess of Egypt discovered Moses, and after his birth mother nursed him to the appropriate age, his adoptive mother, the princess, raised him in the palace. I find it interesting that we have no description of his life in the palace. The book of Exodus simply outlines Moses's next life event.

When the child grew older, she brought him to Pharaoh's daughter, and he became her son. She named him Moses, "Because," she said, "I drew him out of the water." One day, when Moses had grown up, he went out to his people and looked on their burdens, and he saw an Egyptian beating a Hebrew, one of his people. He looked this way and that, and seeing no one, he struck down the Egyptian and hid him in the sand. (2:10–12)

What a life Moses must have lived as for years he peered over walls to see his own people oppressed by the Egyptians! To witness the unfair judgment was too much for his soul. He who had been saved from the hand of the Egyptian king now used his own hands to attempt to balance the scales of justice. Committing murder put Moses on the run from Pharaoh, and he wound up in the wilderness. As the years passed, he eventually settled there and cared for sheep.

One day, in the midst of his shepherd's life, Moses saw a strange phenomenon: a bush engulfed with flames—but without ever burning up! As he drew closer, he heard a voice from within the bush call his name. This was his first personal encounter with the God of the universe.

God's plan was to make Moses the leader of his people and bring the children of Israel out of Egypt. During this first conversation with God, Moses was astounded that God had chosen him to do this, and he drummed up all the reasons he was not the man for the job. He wasn't good enough, no one would believe him, he had a speech impediment, blah, blah, blah. But wait, what was that? No one would believe him?

Hmm, I suppose when you murder someone and cover it up, that would lend itself to making people doubt you. *Just a tad*.

Yet God took Moses through a series of signs and miracles to show him that he was indeed God's man. He had Moses throw his shepherd's staff on the ground and it became a snake. Then God ordered Moses to catch the snake by the tail. Moses did and the snake turned back into a rod. The miracles confirmed what Moses was just starting to understand: regardless of his hang-ups, regardless of his history, it was time for Moses to lose the weight of the past so he could move into the present.

In previous chapters, I mentioned the children of Israel and their forty-year journey through the wilderness. Moses probably didn't know that the steps he took toward the burning bush would change his life forever. Step by step, he would lead the Israelites through faith lesson after faith lesson. He was indeed the leader who did not allow the past to freeze him.

Consistent movement in the present is what propels us toward the future.

As the Israelites wandered for decades, Moses found the strength to take one more step. Though the journey was long, this strength moved the children of Israel to the Promised Land. If Moses would have discontinued his steps, an entire nation could have missed their destination.

Giving Up the Past

When my husband turned forty years old, he began running. I don't mean jogging around the park. I mean the guy started training for his first marathon right out of the gate. Wow, my admiration for his tenacity escalated. As I watched him train and complete marathon after marathon, I felt a little left out. The benefits and habits he established through running were phenomenal. He grew stronger physically and mentally. When I realized the connection between running and his higher-than-normal energy levels, I wanted what he had. Inspired by his efforts, I decided to start running too.

We should pause here so I can tell you that God did not form my legs like my husband's. My husband has tree trunks for legs; I have twigs. I'm just saying. But he was so inspiring that I had to try.

I began running short distances and then worked my way up to a couple of miles. Before I knew it, I was hooked. Running wasn't necessarily fun, but feeling healthy, maintaining a clear mind, enjoying awesome conversations with God while I was running—these were fun! So I kept going until I decided to run my first half marathon: 13.1 miles! Could I really do this?

I knew I could never keep up with my husband; he could run backward faster than I could run forward. But I wanted to do it. I had to do it. So I prepared in advance and printed out a schedule to follow. My list-person attitude kicked in, and I felt so good when I marked off the running goals for each day and week. As time passed, I marked off the schedule and race day arrived. You know what happened? I completed my first half marathon! It wasn't pretty or perfect, but I did it. And it felt incredibly satisfying to accomplish what had seemed to be such a huge goal.

Three half marathons and two babies later, I found myself in training mode once more. Feeling old and slow, I was doing my best to push forward and prepare to run another half marathon. But I couldn't seem to keep going as I had for previous races, and my training list wasn't getting checked off. The weather didn't cooperate, my knee gave me issues, time wasn't on my side, and the excuse list went on. My justifications were valid; I just couldn't seem to get through my list this time.

I muddled my way through the training and completed the half marathon, though not with a personal record by any means. Rain poured throughout the entire race. I don't mean a light sprinkle. For a while, I thought God might have been giving the sign that a second ark should be built. My clothes were soaked, my shoes sopped like ninety-year-old sponges, *and* I was freezing. Every moment of the race was complete misery, from the moment we stepped out of the van to the moment we finished to the moment we stepped back into the van.

While I managed to finish the race, the performance and outcome were flat out ugly. Too many walk breaks, porta-potty stops, and a record low personal time combined to make me feel like a complete and total failure. My poor husband stood in the pouring rain for forty-five minutes, waiting for me to cross the finish line. I felt terrible that he waited so long. Though I hadn't given up, the results were just not what I thought they should be. I had finished this race, but I still wanted to throw in the towel on running any more half marathons.

The day after the race, I told my husband that I wanted to stop running altogether. (He is a patient man.) From the beginning, I hadn't been confident, and feelings of failure invaded my mind. I felt overwhelmed, exhausted, and insecure. While every feeling associated with wanting to give up bombarded my heart and mind, I found myself at a crossroads. My decision wasn't about finding strength to take the next step or beginning to look forward. I had to choose to put the past behind me. The last race? It was over and there was nothing more I could do. But there were still races ahead of me. I had to stop allowing the past to define the future. By latching on to what had happened instead of accepting it, I was holding myself back, and if I camped here and didn't run anymore, I would lose the benefits I had gained thus far. I chose to adopt Abraham Lincoln's philosophy on the issue: "I am a slow walker, but I never walk back."

The Bible tells us that once we accept Christ as our Savior, God does not even remember our past: It says that God "'will remember their sins and their lawless deeds no more.' Where there is forgiveness of these, there is no longer any offering for sin" (Hebrews 10:17–18). **God does not define our future by our past.**

Moses murdered a man, yet God used him to lead the great nation of Israel. God issued Moses the opportunity to step into how he saw Moses as a leader. Even though Moses was convinced he would not be a good leader, he chose to overlook his weaknesses and past mistakes. He chose to follow God's lead in forgetting the past.

If our loving Father can forget our mistakes of the past, then so should we. We may find ourselves looking back occasionally, but when we keep our focus on God's lead, we'll be able to take one more step.

When Giving Up Is Good

Raising the white flag is often viewed as a negative sign. We think of it as the symbol for giving up. After all, a white flag is an internationally recognized signal for surrender. This thought causes us to slap an L-shaped finger and thumb to our heads and label ourselves as losers. Maybe our efforts didn't yield the success we anticipated. Maybe the outcome wasn't what we were looking for, even though we finished the race.

To help me stop dwelling on the things of the past, I wrote down a list of things I would change about the half marathon that made me feel like a failure. Once I identified what they were, I separated the list into two categories: things I couldn't change and things I could change. For example, I couldn't change the weather. But I could change the type of clothing I wore for the race. I continued to write down items in each category, and when I was finished, I crossed out the entire list of things I couldn't change. I created a new set of running goals based on the things I could change. In order to continue running half marathons or any races at all, in order to begin taking a step in the right direction, I had to give up. I had to give up my infatuation with the past. My "failures" could not prevent me from moving forward unless I allowed them to do so.

A few months later, I ran a personal best record for my next race.

By now we've fully recognized that at some time or another, everyone feels like giving up. If you feel like dropping out, you may need to drop your hold on the past. Quit mourning it so you can move into the future with clarity and purpose.

The white flag of surrender is not always a bad thing. The good white flag is the one we raise when we're ready to stop allowing the past to define our present or our future. It's the flag we raise in total surrender to God. This flag signals that we're finished running the show and that we acknowledge our previous mistakes are covered by the blood of Jesus Christ. The awesome part of surrendering our past to the Lord is that even if we can't see the results we've been looking for, we know that God has a plan far greater than we can imagine.

Sometimes we aren't surrendering just the past but also our goals and dreams. All of us dream and make plans in life. But not all of those dreams come to life. As if I need to explain that to you.

I'm a dreamer and always have been. As a child, I got lost in books not only because the characters came to life but also because I could take the characters other places and make up my own stories. I would dream of flying with Amelia Earhart. Annie Oakley and I went on all sorts of adventures together. I was as good a shot as she was. In my dreams.

Taylor has been quite fragile since last autumn. Between seizures and her continual loss of skills as the gradual neurological degeneration infiltrates her brain, she has stayed home from school day after day, and we do our best to hold on to her mobility. She is still breathing on her own and eating by mouth—for this we are thankful and we focus on making the most of each day. But her pace of life is much slower than the rest of the world. I'm learning to appreciate it.

When the diagnosis was issued that Taylor's projected lifespan would be ten to fifteen years, I looked down at her little pigtails and I had a dream. I dreamed that one day she would walk across a platform and receive her high school diploma. Graduation day: Isn't it the pinnacle of the teen years? Doesn't everyone have this dream for her child? And in spite of disease and in spite of her diagnosis, my dream for my girl was that she would graduate from high school. Not with honors or accolades or scholarships, but just the ability to walk and receive a piece of paper that signifies she lived her life to the fullest for the school years allotted to her. Each day she put one foot in front of the other and took one more step.

Since Taylor hasn't been well enough to attend school, at this point we are forced to let a dream die. Due to state regulations and stipulations, I had to make the choice to unenroll Taylor from school. We will never see that dream of Taylor receiving a high school diploma come to fruition. It's a very hard mama place to be. To be honest, Taylor doesn't care. She doesn't know and it does not hurt her feelings because she doesn't understand. It's a strange feeling to be thankful that your child doesn't have enough cognitive ability to know when she's being deprived of a simple joy.

The Lord kept me awake last night because I felt him impressing on me that you too have big dreams and big goals for your life and your children. There's nothing wrong with those big dreams and plans and goals, except that sometimes they are not a part of his plan.

We can't wrap our heads around it; we don't understand all the details. But we can hold on to the promises of God stated by Isaiah: "For my thoughts are not your thoughts, neither are your ways my ways, declares the LORD. For as the heavens are higher than the earth, so are my ways higher than your ways and my thoughts than your thoughts" (55:8–9). **I can take comfort in the fact that God's plan is always bigger and better than mine.**

Redemption is a beautiful word. We often think of *redemption*'s definition as "being freed from sin." God's redemption plan certainly saves us from sin and gives us a home in heaven. We discussed the details of how God performed redemption in the life of Joseph. God's redemption plan also includes taking everything in our past and using it for good in the future.

If we never get to the point of raising the white flag in surrender to God, then we miss the opportunity to see his glorious plan of redemption unfold. Without yielding ourselves to him, we miss out on being free from the past.

I'm stubborn, so for me, it's a process. But giving the past up to God is so much better than missing out on the beauty of tomorrow. I refuse to allow yesterday to define my outlook today. I'd miss a huge opportunity to see what God wants to do right now and in the days ahead if I didn't give MPS up to God.

My bubbly, joyous four-year-old has grown into a beautiful, miraculous eighteen-year-old. We can't change the diagnosis, and the past is what it is. Daily we submit our dreams and goals to our Father who knows best. We are approaching the end of the fight against MPS, and this disease surely has taken a toll on my girl. Although her disease-ridden mind cannot comprehend all of my words, I often say something like this to her:

> Sweet girl, while I had my own dreams and plans for you, God's plan has unfolded day by day in so many more incredible ways than my own dreams ever reached. Your beauty is exquisite and your smile infectious. Your love for life and zeal to press on is an example to all who meet you. I look forward to the day in heaven when you can finally tell me all your thoughts of just how crazy your mama was on this earth. Until then, we continue our best to love God and others, and we take one more step as God gives breath. I love you.

What about you? Have you surrendered to God? How he longs to see your white flag flying high to show him that you are ready to move forward! Let go of the past so you can take steps toward the rewards of the future.

～ ～ ～

Pillars of Truth to Lean On

Need a reminder that the past is in the past? Meditate on this list of verses to find hope for the future.

- Remember not the former things, nor consider the things of old. Behold, I am doing a new thing; now it springs forth, do you not perceive it? I will make a way in the wilderness and rivers in the desert. (Isaiah 43:18–19)

- If anyone is in Christ, he is a new creation. The old has passed away; behold, the new has come. (2 Corinthians 5:17)

- One thing I do: forgetting what lies behind and straining forward to what lies ahead, I press on toward the goal for the prize of the upward call of God in Christ Jesus. (Philippians 3:13–14)

- Since we are surrounded by so great a cloud of witnesses, let us also lay aside every weight, and sin which clings so closely, and let us run with endurance the race that is set before us. (Hebrews 12:1)

Raising the good white flag is ditching the past to promote strength for the present. What do you need to surrender from the past? A situation gone awry, a circumstance you can't change, or a sin God has already forgiven? Craft a few sentences to explain your feelings of giving up and why it is good not to focus on the things you can't change. In your *One More Step* journal, form a written prayer to God surrendering the past, as well as your future goals and dreams. Take your burden to the Lord, leave it there, and turn the page in victory!

sixteen

Finding Joy in Strange Places

Touched by a loving heart, wakened by kindness,
chords that are broken will vibrate once more.

—Fanny J. Crosby

After my husband returned from a worship mission trip to Africa a few years ago, I knew that I too would visit Africa someday. As Matt toured Malawi, he documented his heart through photos and videos. Just seeing his new perspective on life caused me to want what he had experienced. The country is gorgeous and the landscape diverse. The people love to entertain guests and speak graciously. I felt change stirring in me just by witnessing his transformation.

I mentally calculated my "someday" trip to be about ten years into the future. With the house full of children and with Taylor's special needs, it didn't seem likely that I'd be free to go anywhere away from my family for more than a few days.

However, less than two years after my husband's trip, I was presented with an opportunity by Awana International to travel to Africa as a blogger with their global team. The invitation alone made me ecstatic, but I wasn't sure how someone would care for my family in my absence. When I presented the idea to Matt, his first response was that he would take vacation time to stay home with the children so I could go. His huge heart wanted me to experience what he had experienced, and he didn't consider using his vacation time as a sacrifice. You can see why I'm madly in love with him, right? So we set the plans.

Poverty is no stranger to me. I grew up poking around the hollows of West Virginia, playing with barefoot kids who slept with sheep to stay warm at night. I knew a lady who lived in a coal house with no windows and no bed. My dad drove the church bus and helped me understand just how poor folks were, as well as how I should respond to their needs.

I visited the inner city of my college town every weekend and enjoyed conversations with wonderful people of all types. I tasted the best Russian tea I've ever had while visiting a homeless woman. When served by a dear Spanish family, I learned that water and toast can be the most delicious food. I entered houses where roaches covered the walls and I couldn't put my purse down for fear of taking said roaches home with me. Surely all this knowledge and experience would prepare me for a visit to the Kibera slums in Kenya.

And it did in a small-scale way. The house walls were nothing but thin sticks, and the roofs were large dried leaves. I could see through the roof at every shack. Raw sewage runs along both sides of the streets. Everywhere I looked along the neighborhood fences and sides of houses, I could see plastic bags waving in the breeze. The people are afraid to go outside their huts at night to relieve themselves, so they use the bags for their personal needs. In the morning, they dump the human excrement in open ditches alongside the one-way streets and hang up the bag for reuse. Toilets are mere holes in the ground. Water is scarce and must be used sparingly, if you're blessed enough to have access to it. The roads have two conditions: 100 percent dirt or 100 percent mud.

In these surroundings, I was completely and totally unprepared to see the huge smiles on the children's faces. They paid careful attention when I spoke to the group. I told them I have seven children and that I love babies. For the remainder of the visit, they brought babies to me so I could hold them. It was their way of giving me what they knew I loved. They giggled at simple pleasures like a lollipop or pack of Smarties. They laughed at my poor dancing skills.

Unexpectedly, joy radiated everywhere in the midst of devastation.

I have shared with you how important I believe it is to unlock the power of praise, but to see this truth living and breathing in such a contrasting environment astonished me. When we sang together in worship, I knew that the Holy Spirit surrounded us. I could feel the pride of the heavenly Father beaming down on his precious children.

Since I'd never traveled internationally before this trip, the entire mission tour blew me away. I experienced so many different places and people that I felt my senses were heightened the whole time. Though I'm a frugal American shopper, my shopping skills were lacking in Africa. I don't have the chance to practice bartering in the States, so I have a feeling the villagers were happy with my trades. At one stop, while I sat in the backseat of the van, the Maasai tribal women pushed their wares through the side windows, announcing the craft prices. When they saw paper money in our team member's hand, they grew louder and more excited, shouting and throwing hand-carved wooden animals in the van windows. The driver warned them he was pulling away so they would not get injured.

I met a dear pastor and his wife who have served in the slums for twenty years. Their faithfulness and love for the church is remarkable. I loved the ingenuity and creativity of the teachers and students. At one school, two preteen children told the Bible story of Noah and the ark. They had cleverly created an "ark" from recycled trash. When I returned home after the eight-day trip, my heart was love-struck for the Kenyan people.

Now the struggle became what to do with the lessons I'd learned and the lives I had encountered. How could I fathom the massive poverty, much less do anything to help solve the gigantic problem? What did God want me to do about the needs I witnessed? How can one small mama of seven make a difference in a nation of millions living in the slums? Why did God take me on this heart expedition?

Finding Joy

After returning from Africa, I felt dissatisfied with daily life but couldn't pinpoint the reason. For a few weeks, the unsettled feeling in my heart grounded itself by centering on needing less and being thankful for all God had given me, especially the imperfect and tangible. Washing and drying mounds of laundry for my family didn't seem to be all that tough a task. I wasn't washing in the river and using rocks to scrub out dirt. Grocery shopping for my large household didn't seem to be near as much work when I focused on being grateful for easy grocery store access. I realized my blessings and counted them. And upon counting them, God brought me to a new place of understanding.

Joy has nothing to do with location. You can be anywhere at any time. Whether you are in Ohio or Africa doesn't matter. Whether you live in a tiny hut with dirt floors or a suburban house with polished wood floors doesn't matter. You don't have to be in a certain place for joy to flood your soul, because joy is not location-based.

Joy has nothing to do with religion. Relationship with the heavenly Father, not religion, results in joy. Religion offers lists; relationship offers love. I've found that many people practice religion and fewer people promote relationship. Joy is a natural result of fostering a relationship with God.

Joy has nothing to do with economics. The decimal placement in your bank account is no matter. If no amount of money can buy happiness, then you can be sure that no amount of money can buy true joy.

Joy has nothing to do with the size of your sleeping area. You can still praise God when you have no choice but to sleep three children to a twin bed. At one of the orphanages, I asked the children who slept where. They proudly outlined the sleeping arrangements and I boldly asked one little boy with sparkling eyes, "Do you feel crowded?" He quickly replied, "Oh no. They [his bunkmates] keep me warm on cold nights." His joyful outlook took my breath.

Joy has nothing to do with the position of your body and everything to do with the posture of your heart.

I watched as children crammed in together on the floor so their school visitors could use the few chairs in the building. They listened eagerly and paid careful attention to the school headmaster. When he cracked a joke, they laughed heartily. Although I couldn't understand the joke, I laughed at their contagious laughter. A joyful heart can always find a way to laugh.

Giving Thanks

When I feel like giving up and struggle to take one more step, pausing to take inventory on the gratefulness in my heart performs wonders. Taking time to be thankful changes my outlook. Slowing down to reflect on God's gifts rejuvenates my spirit. For me, this inventory on thankfulness and joy holds three questions:

1. What has God done in the past for which I can praise him?
In the moment, difficult circumstances are heavy and burdensome, but looking back at how God delivered me in the past is one way to find joy

in the moment. I think about an answered prayer or a changed situation and I realize God's wonderful work in my life. The memory of what he has done provides hope for the moment, as well as for the future.

When I was pregnant for the fifth time, I worried about affording diapers. I gave the worry over to God many times before giving birth. The week before my daughter was born, God provided diapers in miraculous ways. In fact, we didn't buy diapers for Tarah until she was fifteen months old. I've looked back on his incredible provision dozens of times and thought, *If he cares enough to provide diapers, then I feel confident he cares about* _____.

2. What is God doing in my life right now for which I can praise him?

Even in the toughest circumstances, I can always find something to praise God for. But I have to be willing to open my eyes to more than the immediate. I have to be willing to see from his perspective, with his eyes. Even when I can't find thanks in my heart for what God is doing, I can always find praise for who he is. His love, his faithfulness, his guidance, his unending, never-changing love—these attributes encourage my heart to know that he wants what is best for me.

3. How can I verbalize my joy in anticipating God's plan for my life?

While my spiritual eyesight is often nearsighted, I can tell God how much I love him and trust him. Sometimes it's a simple statement of admission: "God, I can't wait to see what you're going to do, because I know it's going to be good for me and glory for you."

Giving thanks and finding joy is so much more than counting your blessings—although that is extremely important. The next step on a joy expedition is serving right where God has placed you.

Serving

You know, going on a mission trip and serving those less fortunate feels good. It really does. Helping people who have nothing and embracing the opportunity to give to them instigates a heroic spirit within your heart. If you've never experienced it, then it may seem strange to find joy on the faces of orphans living in mud huts.

Pure joy has nothing to do with what you have, but rather who you are and the God you serve.

God hasn't placed my body in a mud hut with raw sewage ditches surrounding it. At least not yet. He placed me in a suburban neighborhood with my awesome husband and six children under our roof, and a daughter and son-in-law living close by. The feeling of heroism I had when I was serving porridge to children in Africa didn't last too long once I had been home for several weeks and adjusted to my own living conditions and life demands. I honestly found myself wanting to give up under the weight of caring for my family and writing this book. (Wouldn't that have been a great ending? What happened to the girl who was writing a book about giving up? Oh, it never happened. She gave up. Whew, the irony.)

All the crazy reasons to give up, which we have processed together through each chapter, washed over me like a tsunami. Then God whispered to my heart:

> *Girl, when you feel like giving up, that is definitely not the time to give up. When you feel like giving up, that is when you need to rely on my strength and remember my promises. The feeling of wanting to give up is temporary; the joy you seek is permanent. True joy is not relevant to physical location or type of service. True joy can be found only in me.*

You see, we lean toward making the effort to heal ourselves. We try every bandage in every color and trick ourselves into thinking that the superhero character on the exterior of said bandage will magically appear in real life and that all will be better. Our brokenness will be healed. The feeling of wanting to give up will vanish and we'll suddenly feel good again. But we must come to the realization that only Jesus, the Savior, Healer, and Redeemer can rejuvenate the broken. The psalmist reminds us that "he heals the brokenhearted and binds up their wounds" (Psalm 147:3).

If that were everything Jesus did for us, it would be more than enough. But his redemptive work does so much more than heal our brokenness.

He takes the feelings of wanting to give up and accepts them for what they are. He lovingly holds our hope and offers a beautiful resting place in his Word. His love surrounds us and provides the strength we so desperately crave. He gives treasures of trust and gifts in the desert wasteland. He helps us grasp that his plan is bigger than ours and provides grace in the moment. He equips us when we're overwhelmed and holds us closely throughout the journey. He forgives us and empowers us to lose the baggage. He shuts down that negative mental ticker tape and strengthens us through his power. He encourages us to sign the dotted line when we "didn't sign up for this." He uses empty heart spaces to bring us to a point of raising the good white flag of surrendering it all to him.

And as if all that weren't far more than we deserve, he gives us the joy-filled opportunity to share the messy brokenness of our lives by serving others. **Jesus not only heals broken hearts, but he also transforms broken hearts into his hands and feet that carry his love and share it with others.** This sharing comes in all forms. Maybe it looks like a cup of cold water to someone in need. Or a pack of Smarties to a precious orphan who needs to see love in action. Or a kiss on my girlie's cheek when her arm needs a cast. Or a love note in my husband's lunchbox. Or the next blog post for some wonderful friends. Whatever shape or form, I know for sure it looks like one more step.

Life is hard. I don't want to leave you on a Pollyanna note that you're going to close this book and all your problems will be whisked away. My sweet girl Taylor is dying little by little, day by day, and life is hardly easy. But Christ who rose from the dead loves both of us, and he has already won the victory. The battle is his, and when I focus on gaining my strength from him, when I believe his Word for what it says, when I rely on his victory, then I find myself strong enough in him to take just one more step. You can too.

Whatever your next step is, God will give you the strength for it.

Blessed be GOD, who has given peace to his people Israel just as he said he'd do. Not one of all those good and wonderful words that he spoke through Moses has misfired. May GOD, our very own God, continue to be with us just as he was with our ancestors— may he never give up and walk out on us. May he keep us centered and devoted to him, following the life path he has cleared, watching the signposts, walking at the pace and rhythms he laid down for our ancestors. (1 Kings 8:56–58, MSG)

～ ～ ～

Pillars of Truth to Lean On

When you're ready for direction for the next step, these verses will bring guidance and strength.

- Only fear the LORD and serve him faithfully with all your heart. For consider what great things he has done for you. (1 Samuel 12:24)

- Where your treasure is, there your heart will be also. (Matthew 6:21)

- Everything created by God is good, and nothing is to be rejected if it is received with thanksgiving. (1 Timothy 4:4)

- God is not unjust so as to overlook your work and the love that you have shown for his name in serving the saints, as you still do. (Hebrews 6:10)

Stepping Stone #16

In your *One More Step* journal, write down three things you can be thankful for when you look at the past and three things you are thankful for in this moment. Write one sentence that helps you understand how these things can help you look toward the future. Where are you serving today? Then list the names of the people or groups you know God has placed in your path. Write down three things you can do to serve these people. Do you know someone who needs some strength because she feels like giving up? If you discovered strength along this journey, share this book.

Discussion Questions

The following questions are intended for deeper personal reflection or can be used to facilitate a four-week small-group discussion.

Week 1

Chapters 1–4

1. Have you ever received permission from a friend to ache freely? If so, how did it make you feel?
2. In which are you most often tempted to rest your hope: things, people, or yourself? What experiences have led you to recognize that's a poor choice?
3. How does the statement "God desires a personal relationship with me—not a religious experience for me" contrast with what you've been led to believe? At the end of chapter 3, which Pillar of Truth to Lean On did you find the most reassuring?
4. Do you find it more difficult to trust God for who he says he is or what he says he will do? Explain your answer.

Week 2

Chapters 5–8

1. If you can, describe a time when you experienced a "gift in the desert." How did chapter 5 help your perspective on times of waiting on God?

2. In chapter 6, did you find yourself shifting your thought process from frustration over not seeing God's work to revelation of his mighty power? If so, what prompted that shift and how is it reshaping your expectations?

3. Is it harder for you to extend grace to others or to receive grace from others? On a scale of one to ten, with ten being the hardest, how hard is it for you to give grace to yourself? Why do you think that is the case?

4. Which tip from David's "Survival Guide" in chapter 8 resonated the most with your overwhelmed heart?

Week 3

Chapters 9–12

1. If you reflect on Christ's forgiveness of your sin, how does that affect your desire to forgive others?

2. When negative internal chatter strikes, how does Philippians 4:8 change your mode of thinking? What is one practical way you know you could stop watering the weeds of your mind?

3. Which type of fatigue do you find yourself battling the most: physical, mental, emotional, or spiritual? When you remember God's inexhaustible supply of strength, how does that affect your mode of operation?

4. Which suggestion to combat loneliness sparked an interest that made you want to follow through on the suggestion? How will you do so this week?

Week 4

Chapters 13-16

1. Do you currently feel that God has given you a task for which you didn't sign up? How did Stepping Stone #13 affect your outlook in this area?

2. What life experiences have left you with a vacancy that can only be filled by Jesus? Have you started to see how these empty spaces can be used by God to connect with others and lead them to him? Explain your answer.

3. When you think of Moses, what word first comes to mind? Do you think of a murderer? Why or why not? How does raising the white flag of surrender on the past give you the encouragement to embrace the present? What dreams have you relinquished for God's ultimate best plan?

4. How have you been inspired through God's Word and this book to pursue a life of joy and thanksgiving by simply taking one more step? How can you share that insight with someone else you know who feels overwhelmed by life?

Acknowledgments

Jesus, how I need you every hour.

My Matthew, God has been so gracious in giving you to me. Thank you for putting up with this melancholy writer as I worked my way through this project. I love you with all my heart.

Tiff and Zach, Taylor, Michael, Tristina, Samuel, Tarah, and Tessa, you are gifts I don't deserve. Each day I'm blessed to call you my children. Thank you for eating Crock-Pot meals and frozen dinners in order to make this book happen.

Dad, you taught me so much and now I'm sharing a speck of your wisdom.

Connie, Kevin, Karen, Chip, Sharon, Philip, Sarah, and Martha, you are the reason I wanted a big family. Life is fun with lots of brothers and sisters to celebrate it with.

Esther, Karen, and Laura, you believed in me when I scarcely believed in myself. God has used you to shape my writing journey and I'm so thankful.

Ginger, thank you for your generous and patient guidance through the editing process.

The Better Mom team and Tommy Mommies team, every blogger needs blogging friends. Thank you for inspiring, encouraging, and listening.

WaterBrook Multnomah teams, thanks for all your hard work and support.

Thoughts to Keep You Going

Chapter 1: Permission to Ache Freely

Recognizing we want to give up is the **first step**
toward **realizing** the pit we're in.

God would **rather hear** about your bad day
than **not hear** from you at all.

Prayer
trumps panic.

Every.

Time.

God **understands**
human emotion
because he **created**
human emotion;
you will never
experience an emotion
that he doesn't understand.

Chapter 2: A Place for Hope

Hope can be placed anywhere we choose, but
the place we choose makes **all the difference.**

When we set our **hope** in people,
we miss the **greatest** source of hope.

Hope in people = Disappointed
Hope in things = Distracted
Hope in ourselves = Devastated
Hope in Christ = Delivered

Only Jesus comprehends **every detail** of what you are going through.

Chapter 3: Love: The Ultimate Pain Reliever

Love **provides** incredible pain **relief.**

We fall in love, trip over it, stumble upon it.
But God? **His path is love** because he is love.

God **desires** a personal **relationship with me— not** a religious experience for me.

Chapter 4: The Buried Treasure of Trusting God

When things seem out of control, God is **always** in control.

Redemption is God **transforming** crazy circumstances into beautiful **blessings.**

Trusting God means you **believe** God is who he says he is and that he will do what he says he will do.

Chapter 5: Gifts in the Desert

The **gifts** we unwrap **in the desert** are often the ones we **appreciate** the most.

Our **focus** is often on the **wait;**
God's **focus** is on the **work.**

The **preparation** God performs in us **equips**
us for the **privileges** he provides.

God alone **knows** when we are **ready for the answer** for which we've been **waiting.**

We want God to give us an **answer;** God wants to give us **himself.**

What we often perceive as **waiting**
is actually God's **wooing.**

Chapter 6: The Purpose Behind God's Plan

Even when bad **things happen** to good people,
God is at work, **orchestrating** his good plans.

I **stopped** asking the question, *God,* ***where are you*** *in all this?* I **started** asking, *God, will you* ***reveal yourself*** *to me?*

If we **trust** God for **eternal salvation,** then let's trust him for **everyday solutions!**

Releasing my grasp of all things temporal allows the grip of God to become **most real** to me.

The God who is **taking us** to heaven
wants to **use us** on this earth.

Chapter 7: The Necessary Grace

Grace takes many shapes, yet one size **fits all.**

The world's **greatest gift exchange**
is humanity's sin for God's grace.

The situations we wish God would remove
from our lives are often the **lessons** God
uses to teach us to **rely** on him.

I realized God wants to
do more than **change
my situation;** he wants
to **change my heart.**

God's immense
grace brings
joy in the
midst of suffering.

Grace is not only a gift from God;
grace is a **gift** to extend to others.

Chapter 8: Overcoming the Overwhelming

Prayer should be our **first response,**
not our **last resort.**

Chapter 9: Ditch Your Carry-on

Our reaction to being wronged is to offer
resentment and rejection. God's response to being
wronged is to offer **resolution and restoration.**

The choice to **forgive** is a choice to **live.**

If only we **freely forgave** with as much strength as we grip grudges.

Chapter 10: Stop Watering the Weeds

True justice is **obeying** God's laws, not merely observing human laws.

God's Word is **the key** to turning negative internal chatter into a disappearing act.

Paul calls us to treat the one teeny tiny negative statement in a sea of **good reports** as the speck of sand that it is.

Praising Jesus overpowers potential negativity!

Chapter 11: Fighting Fatigue

Managing chaos requires more energy than **maintaining rhythm.**

Moving from spiritually exhausted to energetic requires **supernatural strength.**

Executing a to-do list should follow establishing a **to-be list.**

Chapter 12: Someone to Lean On

A kind, open heart is far more **beautiful**
than a harsh, closed mouth.

Chapter 13: Your Signature Here

Working toward a milestone will always
accomplish more than **wishing** for a miracle.

A collection of excuses for why we can't do something
will never evolve into a **treasury** of reasons we did.

Make a memorial when God meets you **miraculously.**

Chapter 14: Sitting on "E"

Emptiness of soul can
be replaced only by
the fullness of God.

God invites us to **look**
beyond the little we have
to the **largeness** of what
he offers.

When we are familiar with God's promises, we can
expectantly appreciate the future.

Sometimes the **boldest** thing we can do
is just take **the next breath.**

Chapter 15: The Good White Flag

We can't allow the desire to change the past freeze our ability to **move** in the present.

Consistent movement in the present is what **propels** us toward the future.

God does not define our **future** by our past.

I can take comfort in the fact that God's plan is always bigger and better than mine.

Chapter 16: Finding Joy in Strange Places

Joy has nothing to do with religion. **Relationship** with the heavenly Father, not religion, results in joy.

Joy has nothing to do with the position of your body and everything to do with the **posture of your heart.**

Pure joy has nothing to do with what you have, but rather who you are and the God you serve.

Jesus not only **heals broken hearts,** but he also transforms broken hearts into his hands and feet that **carry his love** and share it with others.

The Hymns Behind *One More Step*

grew up singing Christian hymns around the piano with my family. The quotes at the beginning of each chapter are lines from the old hymns that I first sang as a young child. The depth of the hymns' words came to life for me when I recommitted to Christ after my divorce. As an avid hymn lover, I wanted to share that deep meaning with you. To enjoy the *One More Step* hymnal, please visit http://rachelwojo.com/onemorestep.

Chapter 1
That Christ hath regarded my helpless estate, and hath shed his own blood for my soul.
"It Is Well with My Soul"—Horatio G. Spafford

Chapter 2
Whispering hope, oh, how welcome thy voice, making my heart in its sorrow rejoice.
"Whispering Hope"—Septimus Winner

Chapter 3
When nothing else could help, love lifted me.
"Love Lifted Me"—James Rowe

Chapter 4
Just from Jesus simply taking life and rest, and joy and peace.
"'Tis So Sweet to Trust in Jesus"—Louisa M. R. Stead

Chapter 5
Let Thy goodness, like a fetter, bind my wandering heart to Thee.
"Come, Thou Fount of Every Blessing"—Robert Robinson

Chapter 6
Never a trial that He is not there, never a burden that He does not bear, never a sorrow that He does not share, moment by moment, I'm under His care.
"Moment By Moment"—D. W. Whittle

Chapter 7
'Twas grace that taught my heart to fear, and grace my fears relieved.
"Amazing Grace"—John Newton

Chapter 8
He is my strength from day to day, without Him I would fall.
"Jesus Is All the World to Me"—Will L. Thompson

Chapter 9
I woke, the dungeon flamed with light; my chains fell off, my heart was free.
"And Can It Be That I Should Gain?"—Charles Wesley

Chapter 10
And while the wave-notes fall on my ear, everything false will disappear.
"Open My Eyes, That I May See"—Clara H. Scott

Chapter 11
Against the foe in vales below let all our strength be hurled.
"Faith Is the Victory"—John H. Yates

Chapter 12

Though sometimes the path seems rough and steep, see His footprints all the way.

"He Keeps Me Singing"—Luther B. Bridgers

Chapter 13

Take my will, and make it Thine; it shall be no longer mine.

"Take My Life, and Let It Be"—Frances R. Havergal

Chapter 14

Little is much when God is in it!

"Little Is Much When God Is in It"—Kittie L. Suffield

Chapter 15

Love so amazing, so divine, demands my soul, my life, my all.

"When I Survey the Wondrous Cross"—Isaac Watts

Chapter 16

Touched by a loving heart, wakened by kindness, chords that are broken will vibrate once more.

"Rescue the Perishing"—Fanny J. Crosby

Additional Information
Regarding MPS and Related Diseases

The following description is an excerpt from the National MPS Society website:

Mucopolysaccharidoses (MPS) and related diseases are genetic lysosomal storage diseases (LSD) caused by the body's inability to produce specific enzymes. Normally, the body uses enzymes to break down and recycle materials in cells. In individuals with MPS and related diseases, the missing or insufficient enzyme prevents the proper recycling process, resulting in the storage of materials in virtually every cell of the body. As a result, cells do not perform properly and may cause progressive damage throughout the body, including the heart, bones, joints, respiratory system, and central nervous system. While the disease may not be apparent at birth, signs and symptoms develop with age as more cells become damaged by the accumulation of cell materials.

For more information, please visit http://mpssociety.org /mps/mps-iii/.

Notes

1. Ann Voskamp, *One Thousand Gifts* (Grand Rapids, MI: Zondervan, 2010), 45.
2. Max Lucado, *Grace* (Nashville: Thomas Nelson, 2014), 98.
3. C. S. Lewis, *The Weight of Glory and Other Addresses* (New York: Macmillan, 1947), 123.
4. *Thayer's Greek Lexicon*, s.v. "of good report," *Blue Letter Bible*, accessed June 5, 2015, www.blueletterbible.org/lang/lexicon/lexicon.cfm?Strongs=G2163&t=KJV.
5. C. S. Lewis, *The Four Loves* (Orlando: Harcourt, 1971), 78.
6. C. S. Lewis, *The Collected Letters of C. S. Lewis,* vol. 3, ed. Walter Hooper (New York: HarperCollins, 2007), 1430.

About the Author

Rachel "Wojo" Wojnarowski is wife to Matt and mom to seven wonderful kids. Her greatest passion is inspiring others to welcome Jesus into their lives and enjoy the abundant life he offers.

As a sought-after blogger and writer, she sees thousands of readers visit her blog daily. Rachel leads community ladies' Bible studies in central Ohio and serves as a creative consultant and speaker. In her "free time" she crochets, knits, and sews handmade clothing. Okay, not really. She enjoys running and she's a tech geek at heart.

Reader, writer, speaker, and dreamer, Rachel
can be found on her website at
www.RachelWojo.com
and on social media at
www.Instagram.com/rachelwojo
www.facebook.com/pages/Rachel-Wojo/180414648720554
www.Twitter.com/RachelWojo
www.Pinterest.com/rachelwojo